WORDPRESS DEVELOPMENT
FOR NOOBS

WRITTEN BY: TIM BROWN

TIMBDESIGN.COM

TECHNICAL EDITOR: BRENNEN PHIPPEN

EDITOR: LIZ LORGE

LAYOUT ASSISTANT: DAMIAN KIRCHOFF

ISBN-13: 978-1539956037
ISBN-10: 1539956032

TABLE OF
CONTENTS

INTRODUCTION

WordPress Development for Noobs is a short book where I will explore creating a WordPress website from the ground up, with an eye on people who have little to no WordPress development experience. As a web developer in Minneapolis, I get a lot of questions about this and also appreciate sharing what I've learned, particularly because many people might not know, there is quite a bit you can do on your own if you're willing to invest a bit of time.

Thank you to Brendon for editing this for technical WordPress related elements, Liz for editing it for grammar and spelling, and Damian for assisting me in getting it laid out for print.

And most of all — thank you for reading this. I assure you I tried to boil this book down to the essence of what I felt like I would have appreciated when I just got started — there's nothing crazy in depth here but there are some real takeaways that will help you get up and running much quicker than I did.

And if you have a question — StackOverflow and Google are your friends and there is no shame in using their power.

Good luck and Godspeed.

CHAPTER ONE

HOW TO INSTALL WORDPRESS
FOR THE FIRST TIME

How to install WordPress on common hosting accounts such as GoDaddy, HostGator or BlueHost.

If you are getting into WordPress and possibly even web development for the first time, you may be a little bit intimidated by installing WordPress from scratch. But it is so simple. And with WordPress, web development can be almost as simple as you want it to be, but the first step has a couple moving parts to it. This is true particularly if you want to do it from scratch on your webhost and not use a one-click WordPress install solution. Once you follow the steps here, you are one big step toward becoming something very useful indeed; a WordPress Wizard.

 1. Download WordPress:

It's as simple as it sounds! Just head on over to WordPress.org and download the most recent version of WordPress. WordPress.org is centered around the open source version of this powerful content management system, whereas WordPress.com is about using it more as a blogging tool and because they host it, there are very big limitations to that route.

When you download the most recent version from WordPress.org, feel free to unarchive the file as it will download as a zip file.

 ## 2. Create a Database on Your Hosting Account:

Of course you'll need to HAVE a hosting account in the first place, so head on over to GoDaddy, BlueHost, HostGator, or A Small Orange to get your hosting account first if you haven't. I am satisfied with the hosting I have with GoDaddy, but there are many strong opinions on the matter, so feel free to read up. Make sure to choose hosting that gives you the appropriate amount of databases for your needs. Each new website you create using WordPress or any 'content management system will require another database.

Here is an image showing where you might find your databases in your hosting account. **A. Any hosting account using CPanel. B. GoDaddy Hosting.**

For GoDaddy Hosting: Press "Add a Database."

MANAGE DATABASES

Fill out the fields and remember (or jot down) your information–
you'll need it for the next step.

ADD A MYSQL DATABASE

Set up a database for your data driven or data collection site.

* Required

MYSQL VERSION

○ 5.5 (recommended)
○ 5.1

FRIENDLY NAME ⓘ

DATABASE NAME AND USERNAME * ⓘ

NEW PASSWORD *

CONFIRM PASSWORD *

OK   Cancel

For CPanel: Press "Create New Database."

Fill out the fields for your database, and jot down the
information.

Create a new username and password and jot them down, as you will need this information in the next step.

MySQL Users
Add New User

Username:	mrb_
Password:	
Password (Again):	
Strength (why?):	Very Weak (0/100)	Password Generator

Create User

For CPanel: On the next page, you can manage the privileges for the user. You need to ensure you give your user "All Privileges" as it allows WordPress to modify the database, create new tables, execute and more.

 3. Upload WordPress via an FTP Manager

If you don't have one yet, there are some great free FTP file managers such as FileZilla. Simply install the FTP manager, and connect to the your hosting via an FTP user you can create in your hosting account. **Follow the link to the video below** shows which shows the process of creating an FTP user that you can use to access the files in your hosting account via FileZilla or a similar FTP file manager.

bit.ly/ftp-user ▷

Press "File > Site Manager" and enter your info as shown in the image below. Enter your host (the host you've set up your FTP username under,) choose "Use Plain FTP" next to "Encryption" and then Login Type of "Normal." Enter your FTP user and password.

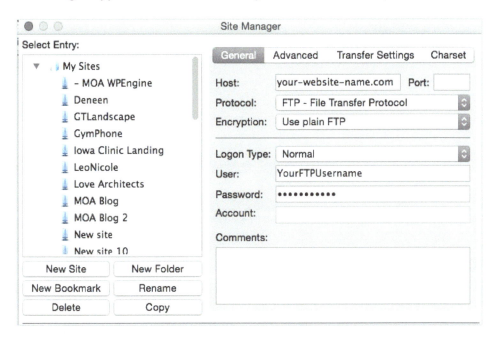

If you want to install WordPress on the root of the domain, highlight all the files within the WordPress file you downloaded from WordPress.org, and drag them into the root file that you have open in your FTP manager. The root of the domain means as the main site for your account – for instance, the root of my domain is timbdesign. com, a subdirectory is timbdesign.com/test. If you want to upload it in a subdirectory, simply name the WordPress file whatever you'd like the subdirectory to be and upload the full thing via the FTP manager. I will often hook the domain name up to it, and because I have a larger hosting account I can keep adding dot com's in the hosting account, and they each have their own WordPress install.

So in that case, rename the WordPress file, like the one circled in this screenshot, to the subfolder name of your choice, then drag it into the FTP manager.

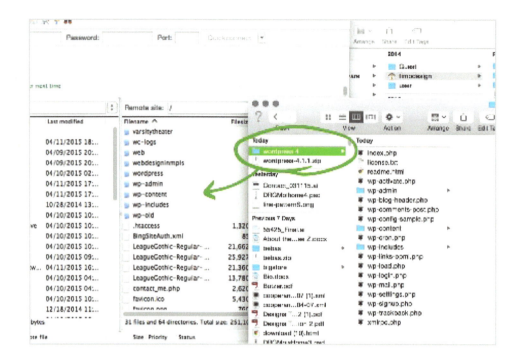

 Now Run the "5 Minute Install":

Navigate to the home domain if you uploaded the guts of the WordPress file to your root, or navigate to the subfolder if you renamed the WordPress file and uploaded it.

Here you can go ahead and press "Create a Configuration File."

There doesn't seem to be a `wp-config.php` file. I need this before we can

Need more help? We got it.

You can create a `wp-config.php` file through a web interface, but this do safest way is to manually create the file.

Create a Configuration File

On the next screen you can enter the information you wrote down earlier (database name, database username and password, database host, and table prefix). Simply click on the "Let's go" button. Next you will see the form to enter all the information.

Below you should enter your database connection details. If you're not sure about these, contact your host

Database Name	wordpress	The name of the database you want to run WP in.
User Name	username	Your MySQL username
Password	password	and your MySQL password
Database Host	localhost	You should be able to get this info from your web host. If `localhost` does not work
Table Prefix	wp_	If you want to run multiple WordPress installations in a single database, change this

After you type in the information, click "Submit." It will take you to the page that has the button to "Run the Install." Click on it.

On the following screen, you will see the form to enter your website's information. This information would be your site's title and your username, password and email.

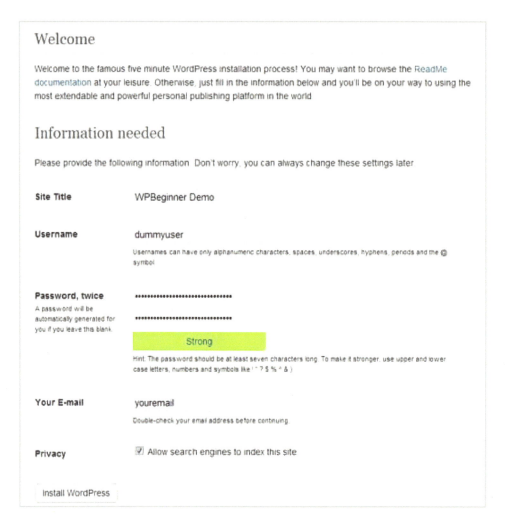

Click Install WordPress, and you have entered a new realm of knowing how to install WordPress, which is a pretty cool place to be.

Options for installing WordPress with a one-step install, such as WPEngine or GoDaddy's dedicated WordPress hosting, and reviews of each.

Don't want to do all that finagling? Well, with the ease of use of new WordPress Managed hosting, and the wonderful people they seemed to copy (WPEngine), you can quickly be up and running without ever even laying one eye on a "Database."

GoDaddy One-click Install

For GoDaddy Managed WordPress Hosting, you simply choose a WordPress hosting plan and it's already been installed for you. All you have to do is set up your website.

First, login to your GoDaddy account. You will see a Web Hosting toggle in your Products tab. Open it up and click the "Launch" button for your new hosting plan.

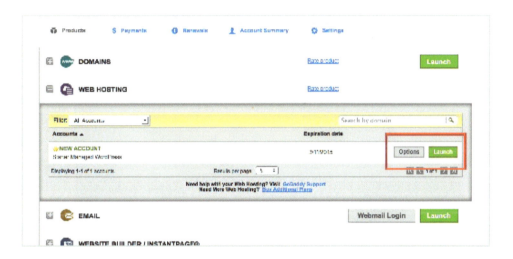

Next you'll need to create your website, or migrate a site you've already created. For this walk-through, we chose to set up a new site to show you all of the options GoDaddy has to offer.

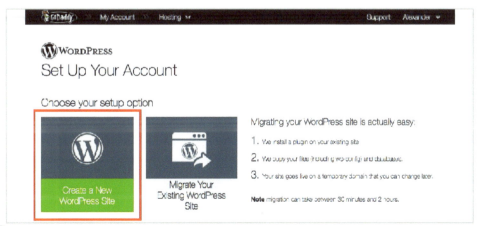

When you choose to create a new WordPress site, GoDaddy gives you a quick form to fill out. You should have already purchased a domain name for your website, and if you purchased it from GoDaddy, just select it from the dropdown. If you do not have a domain yet, use the temporary domain option (GoDaddy will assign a random staging domain name for you to use). Then add in your admin account information and click "Finish."

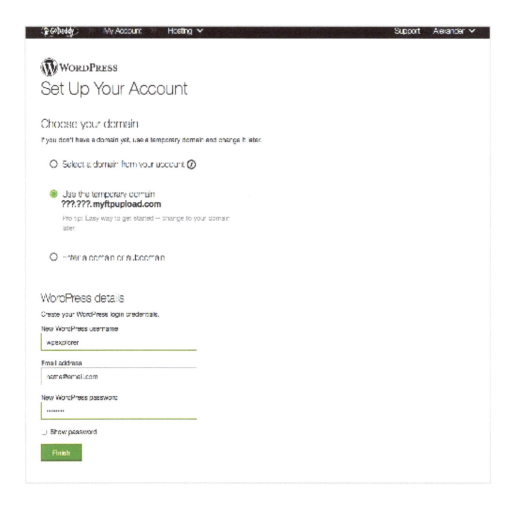

As soon as you click that button, GoDaddy gets to work creating your website, and in just a few minutes or less you'll see your brand new dashboard.

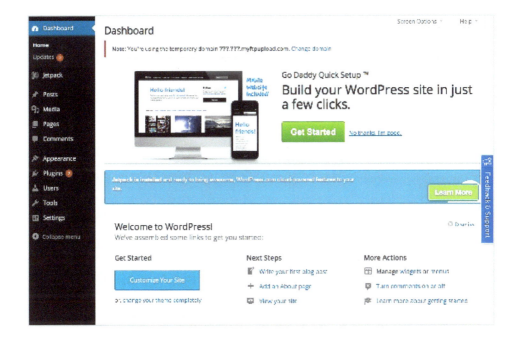

From here you have two options: Either click on the big green "Get Started" button for GoDaddy Quick Setup, or upload and install your own theme and plugins.

 WPEngine Simple Installs:

If you have a pro account with WPEngine, you will be able to add multiple WordPress installs to your account. You can't delete the initial install that was created when you first set up your account with WPEngine. For them, your account is set up under URL account_ name.wpengine.com and cannot be deleted. You can add and delete installs within their User Portal.

To Add an install, log into their user portal and click on "Installs" in the top nav bar:

Then click on "Add Install" in the left nav bar under your current install(s):

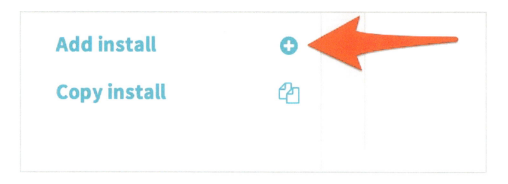

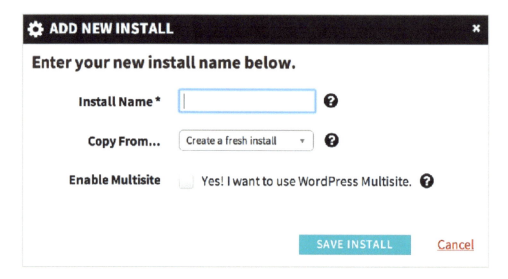

Type in the name of your install, then click on the button that says "Save Install."

You will receive an email shortly, notifying you that your install has been created.

 GoDaddy vs. WPEngine vs. BlueHost vs. ???? :

I can speak to GoDaddy's dedicated hosting, and WPEngine's, from first-hand experience as well as thoughts from around the web about people's experience using BlueHost's one-click install hosting.

GoDaddy seems to have taken a clue from WPEngine's very dedicated WordPress hosting and given people more of a WordPress-specific hosting backend. wWhen you are signed into their dedicated WordPress hosting, everything is very visual and cleaned up from past years before dedicated hosting. This has always been the case for WPEngine as they are bit fresher on the scene in general.

WPEngine is a little bit more expensive, and it's assumed that you may have a bit more riding on your website. There is a staging and production version of your site and you are able to keep it backed up in that way all the time while developing. If you ran into a hiccup while uploading a plugin or writing in your functions.php file (a critical file that helps define some key things for WordPress themes) you can have a snapshot of the website backup the work you've been doing and avoid what WordPress developers have called "The White Screen of Death."

Both of these services are very fast and extremely easy to set up. You can also tell that this is a lucrative business, because both WPEngine and GoDaddy customer service are very much on their game as of late. **This is no Comcast. These people do make it seem like they care.**

From what I can tell, WPEngine is the more premier version with its backup system, but GoDaddy is a great solution as well.

 Other Options:

I am apt to include some thoughts on BlueHost here as well, because they have been endorsed by WordPress, though it seems some think that this endorsement may be highly biased because of sponsorship. However, after looking into BlueHost's WordPress one-step install, it looks as though configuration is very simple indeed. Just consider that many people have cited down-time and speed issues, but there doesn't seem to be a shortage of at least some people with these types of issues with many hosting solutions out there.

There are many one-click install solutions out there, and although security may have been a concern at one point for these solutions, they are becoming more so. Just make sure to change passwords during the process away from default passwords, and make them long and hard to break.

 How to install WordPress without hosting on your computer locally, for development purposes.

I may be in the minority of web developers, but I don't mind developing on a hosting account directly, but a lot of developers swear by developing on WAMP, MAMP, Desktop Server or LAMP. These all allow you to develop your websites that require a database (WordPress or any website with a content management system) on your computer without it being live on the web.

 This video quickly shows how to easily use MAMP (Mac) but its principles apply directly to WAMP (Windows) and LAMP (Linux) as well.

I can speak to GoDaddy's dedicated hosting, and WPEngine's, from first-hand experience as well as thoughts from around the web about people's experience using BlueHost's one-click install hosting.

bit.ly/mamp-wordpress

Now that you have WordPress installed on your site, the next chapter will go over things to do as soon as you have WordPress installed, and some basics of working in WordPress.

CHAPTER TWO

THINGS I DO AFTER I FRESHLY INSTALL WORDPRESS

AND WORDPRESS BASICS

 What common plugins you might like to install on a fresh install of WordPress and how to adjust some basic settings

A "plugin" is a quick way to increase the functionality of your WordPress content management system. After you've installed WordPress on a one-click install, or downloaded it from WordPress. org through connecting it to a database, you might benefit from the plugins I'm about to share with you right out of the gate. It's important to note that some plugins can affect the speed of your website, so use them sparingly and only when they really add value to the site. Here are some basic settings that might be good to adjust after a fresh install of WordPress as well as some of the best paid plugins for WordPress development.

To install a plugin in WordPress, simply click on Plugins > "Add New" in the left-side menu and either search for a plugin there or press "Upload Plugin" to upload one that you have downloaded.

 1. Yoast SEO for Search Engine Optimization/ Being as visible as possible on search engines like Google:

Yoast SEO is an incredibly useful plugin that allows people to quickly affect how each web page shows up on Google. Yoast WordPress SEO creates a sitemap and create an XML sitemap for the purpose of helping Google's crawling function find its way around your site quickly and effectively. It also gives you ways to directly affect the way your site is served in each SERP (search engine results page). You can enter information how you want each page to be served to

Google while you're entering the content for those pages, as shown below, and optimize it around particular keywords. Yoast will nudge you to make sure you represent your keywords in key places that represent what the post is about. It's a handy function indeed.zip file.

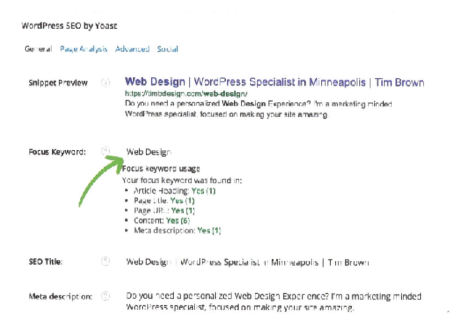

An example of how the site would then show up in the search engine results page:

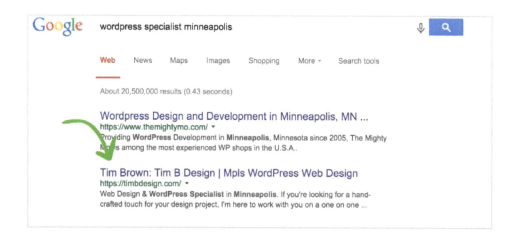

Jetpack (by the people who maintain WordPress, Automattic) for quick stats, automatic social posting and spelling and grammar help:

Jetpack has some intensely useful features, but a couple that strike me as most immediately useful are.. **Site Stats:** Site Stats quickly and painlessly allow you to look at how many pageviews you have gotten today, this week, and this month. I currently am using Google Analytics, but out of the gate it's great to be able to see what pages are attracting eyes. **Publicize:** You can quickly set up automatic sharing on Facebook, Twitter, LinkedIn, and Google Plus. Spelling and **Grammar Checker:** Don't tell me you never misspell anything. This feature helps you stay on your toes when it comes to those pesky little writing mistakes.

Best paid or advanced plugins that really expand functionality for WordPress developers:

Because I will touch on these later in this book, I will be somewhat brief here.

Advanced Custom Fields for developers allows you to give the business-owner or whoever will be entering content into the site "fields" that tell them exactly what they need to enter when they are editing a particular page, and then you can put them into the template for the page with an easy-to-use hook. The premium version is $100 dollars for the unlimited sites, or $25 for a single site.

WooCommerce quickly helps you set up a store on your website. It installs the necessary pages right out of the gate, and let's you add and sell products. The default payment gateway is PayPal, but you can hook up Authorize.net among others and take credit cards right on the site. If you do, just make sure to purchase an SSL Certificate from your hosting provider so that the transactions are secure. WooCommerce is a free plugin, but sells premium add-ons to its users who expand its functionality.

Gravity Forms helps you build contact forms in a very intuitive way, and it has a ton of options and add-ons for making your forms do almost anything you could hope for including quickly displaying more fields if a particular checkbox is checked. If you're a person creating a lot of websites and see how valuable this incredibly functional plugin is, the Premium Version with unlimited sites is $199, or for one site it's $39 as of this writing.

Some of these premium plugins, particularly the ones mentioned above, are worth their weight in gold, (or days of writing code) so don't shy away from spending a little money. You have to spend money to make money.

 Settings to adjust as soon as you install WordPress:

Delete any auto-generated posts and pages: Click on "pages" in the left sidebar of your WordPress admin when you're signed in and hover over "Sample Page," then click "delete." Click on "posts" in the right sidebar of your WordPress admin when you're signed in and hover over the "Sample Page," then click delete.

Change your "Permalink" structure so your URLs look nicer. When you install WordPress, the default permalink structure is like http://yourwebsite.com/p=123 – this permalink is really not very friendly for search engines. It's smart to change it to make it more search engine friendly. Go to settings > Permalink, and select the setting to use post name and click on "save."

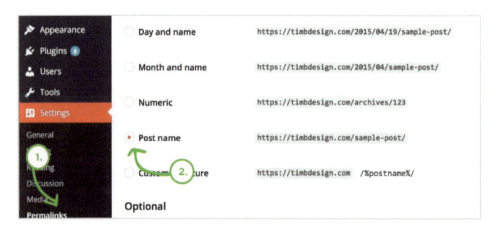

Adjust your general settings; set your tagline and make sure your timezone is correct. 1. Click on "Settings", "General." 2. Change site, title and tagline to help people better recognize what your website is about. You may want to get into slogans here, but I prefer being descriptive first before getting cute for the sake of helping search traffic find me when they are actually looking for something like me. 3. Change the timezone so that anything on your site that uses this setting, like post dates and WordPress stats, on your blog is accurate. So, since I do WordPress development in Minneapolis, Minnesota, you can see I chose the Chicago timezone.

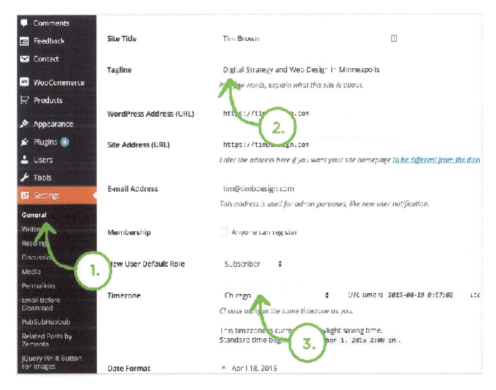

For first-time WordPress Users: How to create posts and pages in WordPress, Add Media, featured images, and other WordPress basics.

22

Creating a post in WordPress:

There are a couple basic things that are not super hard to do, but you have to learn to walk before you can run. I know that even when I first signed into WordPress for the first time, I didn't know how to create a post. Here's a screenshot of how you will create your first post.

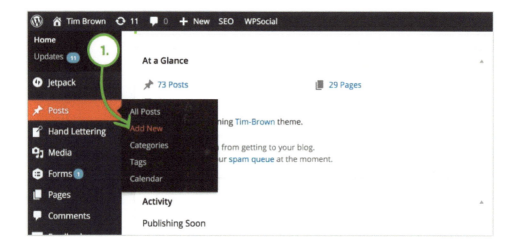

Here's a screenshot of how you will create your first page:

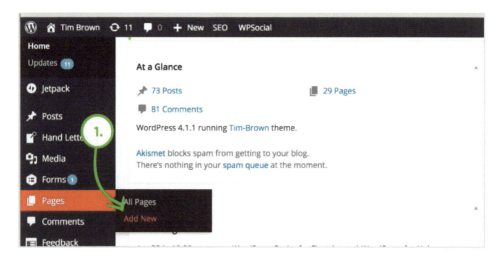

The difference between posts and pages:

A page is generally composed of static content: Think... the about page or a contact page. Whereas a post is generally something that you spin up like a blog article; it's built so that you can quickly put out one of them. You can add them with different categories, and there is often a listing page that allows someone to sort through them and choose one they would like to read. If you are a developer, just know that the blog article PHP loop is a very useful one when you start to create listing pages and pieces of content where you want to show multiple items.

The WordPress Loop allows you to show however many of the posts you want, and the kind of posts you want to show based on categories and tags. More on this later but for now, know that whether you are creating and working on a post or creating and working on a page, many of the things you will be doing to create and format either are very similar. Follow along with these steps to create your first post or page.

 Adding your WordPress post or page for the first time is a bit like working on a word document: Don't be intimidated:

1. Add a title. **2.** Change the URL if you want it to be different than the title (maybe shorten it for easy sharing). **3.** Add some paragraph text, and break up your paragraphs with headings, such as a "Heading 2" by selecting "Heading two" from the editor's text format dropdown as shown. This is a great feature for breaking up the text for easy scannability in your pages and posts.

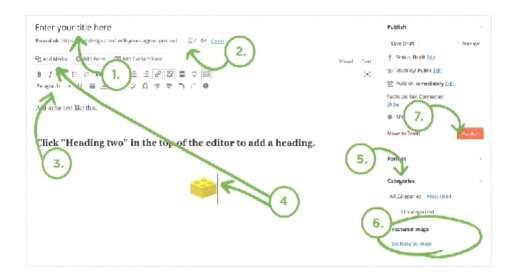

4. Press "Add Media" to add an image to your post. You will be able to drag a photo into the "insert media" box or select a previously uploaded image. Select the alignment of the image (so the text will wrap) perhaps unselect the option to "link to the selected media file," and select the size of the image you would like. WordPress automatically creates different sizes of the image for you, which is a great feature. **5.** Select any categories you would like the post to be listed as or "+ Add New Category." **6.** Select an image to represent the post on social media, and to represent it on main blog listing pages for posts. **7.** Press "publish," and press "view post" to check your work and make sure things are looking right.

For first-time WordPress users or developers: Installing a theme and creating a child theme.

If you are not planning on getting into WordPress development, the main thing you'll need to know is how to install a theme. I'd like to tell you that if you install a theme that everything will be taken care of for you. But it may take some time for you after that to get the theme configured and the website looking right for your purposes. WordPress has a ton of power and can connect to a lot of backend systems that small– to medium-size businesses may need. If, like me, you've come to the conclusion that WordPress is more powerful for your purposes, consider looking at the top premium WordPress themes on ThemeForest.

 What is a theme?

I can speak to GoDaddy's dedicated hosting, and WPEngine's, from first-hand experience as well as thoughts from around the web about people's experience using BlueHost's one-click install hosting.

 Installing a WordPress theme for the first time:

To install a WordPress theme, hover over "Appearance" in the left side menu and click "Themes." If you've found the WordPress theme you want, click "Add New" toward the top left, then "Upload Theme" in the same spot on the screen after that. You will then upload the theme that you've downloaded. Alternatively, you could search the free themes that are listed when you pressed "Add New," but with a lot of free themes, you get what you pay for. Basically, I'm saying if you're a small business owner, or something like that, and not a developer, buy a theme and pay for a nice one. You'll likely save yourself time and headaches.

 If you are going to be editing the theme you choose (usually this would mean you are developer,) make sure to make a child theme:

A child theme allows you to edit the templates of the theme, and the site will use your edited template only if you have a file named the same thing as the same file in the main theme folder. Developers; you can find the theme template folders in "yourwebsite/wp-content/themes/themename". Some of the key files for WordPress are "functions.php", "header.php", "footer.php", "index.php", "page.php", and "single.php". I will go into more detail of these files in the following chapters. If you are looking to get into WordPress theme development, I think it's often a good idea to edit a couple themes that other people created first.

Creating a child theme:

If I wanted to edit the "header.php" file of a theme, I would copy it into my child theme. You could have your theme in the file "yourwebsite/wp-content/themes/themename-child." It should have a style sheet called "style.css" with this at the top:

```
1
2    /*
3        Theme Name:        Theme Name Child
4        Theme URI:         https://www.timbdesign.com/theme-page
5        Description:       The child theme for "Theme Name"
6        Author:            Tim B Design
7        Author URI:        https://www.timbdesign.com
8        Template:          themename
9        Version:           1.0.0
10   */
11
12   @import url("../themename/style.css");
13
14   /* =Theme customization starts here
15   -------------------------------------------------------- */
16   |
```

You'll want to add an image to the file where you have your child theme named "screenshot.png" and it should be 600 x 450 pixels. I like to have this image be a picture of how the site will look (maybe the mockup.) Then when the site is developed, I can take an actual screenshot of the home page and have it occupy this space. As you can see, I've used this in a computer mockup image in the example below for my own site.

When you have your style.css file in your folder you can now go to "Appearance > Themes" and activate the child theme.

Next in the "WordPress for Noobs" series we will talk about utilizing theme options, take some strong steps in learning how to modify theme templates, and start on the basics of creating a WordPress theme "from scratch."

bit.ly/mamp-wordpress

CHAPTER THREE

WP THEMES: WHEN TO USE THEME OPTIONS
AND WHEN TO CODE

 What are theme options and how do they work?

Theme options are different from theme to theme in WordPress, but they are places where the original developer of a site tried to give as much functionality at the fingertips of the end user of the site as possible. In theme options at a basic level, you might have access to background colors, the size and colors of heading text and other text, and up to and including how menus show up or whether or not to use a boxed layout or even full-width layout.

Below is an example of what theme options might look like. They could be called simply "Theme Options" or something to that effect.

In the picture above, you can see that so many things are available to give colors and define options so that the website looks more like you want it to to. The theme dynamically pulls this info in via the database where it's saved and the coding language PHP defines these colors and functions so that the website shows up differently.

Don't think that utilizing theme options will take you all the way if you have a specific visual design goal in mind:

Likely, you will still have to write custom code and lots of it to really get the look you're going for if you have a specific end visual look you'd like because theme options can only really bring you so far. Use them, but they really are intended for a non-developer client or someone running a small blog. Thus, most theme modifications take significant diligence to write custom CSS (Cascading Style Sheets – which style the look of a site,) and modify PHP templates heavily.

 Utilize a base/simple theme if deeper theme options and structure are getting in your way. Developers often find having a simple but solid theme structure to start can help speed up their development.

The key is that when you start to modify templates so heavily the theme is getting in the way more than helping is when you should consider starting from scratch. If you do go this route, might I suggest Underscores? This base theme with no styles was created by Automattic, the people that who to WordPress as a whole, so it's well written but also very simple. I will be sharing a version of Underscores, with Bootstrap built in an upcoming post in this series. Sometimes it's nice to start with something with very few predefined options and structure, because it's easier to bend to your will. Or it might be worth the investment of time to build your own starter theme that you're very familiar with so that you can modify it quickly for the task at hand.

 When I'm modifying a theme, when should I try to use the pre-built options?

If you are using a theme with deep options like this, use the theme options for as many things as possible before moving to custom code.

If you have chosen a theme that gives you access to all of these things, I think of it as a very smart idea to keep as much of this intact as possible. If you have a theme with deep options like this, coding over these styles when it's not necessary means you'll have redundant code, and if someone (like the client, or the client's buddy) is trying to edit the site later via these options, they will be frustrated. Why not use as many as possible and keep the theme functioning at it's highest caliber?

Go down the list and reference your visual design, defining as many of the options as possible based on the design:

It's worth it to go down all of the options in the theme while looking at the visual design and defining all the styles available according to the Photoshop, Illustrator or Sketch document. Check for these options both in a link on the sidebar that says something like "Theme Options" and in the top navigation the theme customizer, under the item "Customize." This way, once you define every possible option available, you can code the rest of the things with full confidence you're not overruling styles unnecessarily.

When I've exhausted the options of a theme, how do I get down and dirty to modify the theme. Where do these functions exist in the site?

Go down the list and reference your visual design, defining as many of the options as possible based on the design:

1. Click "editor" under appearance.

2. Click the template you want to edit.

3. Edit the raw code in the editor.

You can also edit your files by signing into an FTP editor on your site and navigating to the root folder of the site, then go to >wp-content > themes > theme-name, and of course, if you read the last article about WordPress basics, you've created a child theme and copied any files you want to modify into it, so you might navigate to the 'theme-child' folder. Some of the most important files to start looking at right away are the 'header.php', 'footer.php', and the 'functions. php' templates. The header and footer files are used by every page on your site, so you can edit them once and it changes for every page.

 Here is a video showing you how to edit a website's files via FTP:

bit.ly/filezilla-setup

 You can also edit your code with a couple other methods in the WordPress admin as well. The plugins "WPide" and Jetpack's Custom CSS, both give you quick ways to edit code:

If you have Jetpack installed, you can go to Appearance > Custom CSS and add custom CSS styles there, which can come in handy if you've decided to use your CSS this way. Jetpack saves every version of your CSS, so you can go back to a previous version whenever you want, which is nice. There is also a plugin called "WPide" which allows you to dig into a theme, and actually edit any part of your WordPress site via the WordPress admin, whereas standard WordPress file editor only allows you to edit themes.

CHAPTER FOUR

MODIFY WORDPRESS THEMES CODE:
SOME BASICS

What are the main templates I'll need to start editing when I want to make changes my theme doesn't allow? Here are a couple examples of key changes you might want to make.

If you've exhausted your theme options, don't despair! There are a couple key templates you'll want to edit. In the last chapter, we discussed how to edit the key files after you exhaust theme options. But let's dive into why you'd want to edit header.php, footer.php or other files.

If you want to make a change to the top areas of your website that your theme doesn't allow, likely you'll be making the change in header.php:

Before you get started, be sure to duplicate the theme folder and create a "child theme" folder and copy the files you are going to change into it based on the instructions here in a previous chapter.

For the sake of keeping certain things consistent across a whole website and not having to make a change 10 – 20 times or more, editing header.php will make changes site-wide. Usually it's reserved for things like the logo, the menu and other elements at the top of the site. So, for instance, if we wanted to add the phone number for the company to the top of the site, but the theme didn't have an option for this, I might go into the header.php file (under the right-side menu "Appearance > Editor" or in the site files under 'wp-content/themes/theme-name/') and edit the code there. Add it where it would make sense, perhaps before both the logo and the menu.

The HTML:

```
1   <div>
2       <span class="phone-span">Questions? Call us at:
3           <span class="phone-number">1(800)-555-5555</span>
4       </span>
5   </div>
```

The CSS:

```
1   .phone-span {display: inline-block; float: right; color: #333;}
2   .phone-number {font-size: 1.3em; clear: both;}
```

This is just an example. Likely if you're reading this book all the way through you're already somewhat familiar with code, but if you're just referencing this to do one particular thing, maybe you need a bit of understanding of how HTML and CSS work. HTML is the structure, and CSS is the styling element in this instance. You will also encounter PHP while editing your WordPress site, but let's not worry too much about that for the moment. The idea here is not to get too intimidated at this point and just avoid editing the PHP that currently exists in your theme.

WordPress PHP is generally fairly simple and there is so much documentation about how to make changes effectively via the codex and WordPress forums that if you have the attitude that you're ready to learn, and you know that it may take some time, you'll be pleased at how much progress you can make relatively quickly with a little bit of savvy Googling.

 The WordPress loop calls in content from the admin for easy content editing, and the structure of the page outside of this is made in templates like page.php. Make structural changes in these templates so people editing content don't have to worry about messing up the structure of the site.

For the time being, let's look at another change you might make as you dive into code. Once again, since we're talking about modifying a theme, make sure your theme doesn't have an option for this already. I often like to add a call-to-action section to the inner pages of the websites I'm working on. So for many of them, this template, the "guts" (not the header or the footer), of this inner page is editable through the template page.php.

Your WordPress site might be using something more custom like right-sidebar.php or page-content.php, but you can often tell by right clicking on the page you want to edit and checking the "body class." Go to the tag <body> and if your theme is using the WordPress loop for displaying the body classes, there would be something that tells you what PHP template you can edit to change that page. It might say something like inner-page-php as a class and then you'd know that the template you'd need to edit would be inner-page.php.

The template structure often wraps the WordPress loop.

```
1
2    <div class="content-wrap">
3        <?php the_content('') ?>
4    </div>
5
```

The WordPress loop in a template is where the content that you enter into the WYSIWYG (or "what you see is what you get") editor will show up within the template. Using that area is great for things that will change from page to page, but things you want to add to every page should be done within the template. Also for the sake of making the site easy to edit and not easy to break, it's important to put wrappers, divs and other structural elements outside of the WYSIWYG. Otherwise why use a content management system if a client needs to be afraid of breaking their site by editing their content? In a couple chapters we'll discuss how to add multiple areas a client could edit in the WordPress admin and making them show up in a template. But, back to the challenge at hand: adding a section below the content on your page template.

Here's how you would add a call-to-action section to your main inner page template.

So let's say we're in page.php, which is the default page template usage in WordPress. You'd add a div (a div is an HTML element that is used to block out different elements on a page) after the content and any wrapper divs (a wrapper div might be a div element that is used to contain a block, or span the full width of a page) existed to encapsulate the content, like so:

```
1
2   <div class="full-width-cta-wrap">
3       <h3>Like what you see here?</h3>
4       <strong>Contact us to get started</strong>
5       <a class="big-orange-button" href="#contact_form">Let's Work Together</a>
6   </div>
7
```

Yep! You need to style that in your style.css file, too! Here's an example:

```
1
2    .full-width-cta-wrap {
3        width: 100%;
4        display: block;
5        clear: both;
6        padding: 50px 0;
7        text-align: center;
8        background-color: #01404f;
9        margin: 40px 0;
10   }
11
12   .full-width-cta-wrap h3 {
13       color: white;
14   }
15
16   .full-width-cta-wrap strong {
17       color: white;
18       clear:both;
19       display: block
20   }
21
22   .big-orange-button {
23       clear: both;
24       padding: 20px 50px;
25       margin: 20px 0;
26       border-radius: 5px;
27       background-color: #e88400;
28       color: white;
29   }
30
31   .big-orange-button:hover {
32       background-color: #c16f02;
33   }
34
```

Let me show you how that would look on a site:

I usually like to make this section full-width, so at the bottom of the template I'd make sure it was outside the div of the content wrapper (here it's inside for efficiency). Your fonts might look different, of course, as your site is likely loading different ones. One other key change you'd make is, you'd want to put your contact page link in the href= section. Perhaps href="/contact".

 For first-time WordPress Users: How to create posts and pages in WordPress, Add Media, featured images, and other WordPress basics.

HTML and CSS take time to learn, but here are some quick tips if you're just getting started:

The official definition for HTML is: "HTML is a markup language for describing web documents (web pages). HTML stands for Hyper Text Markup Language." HTML is the standard for setting up the structure of web pages and often languages are used to generate HTML, but a lot of what you see on the web is rendered in HTML. For instance, in WordPress, PHP allows you to offer an editor up to the person using the website, and the content they enter is stored in a database and populated in the template on the front-end. Understanding this will help you wrap your mind around editing WordPress templates efficiently.

Similarly, JavaScript or Jquery elements are added and referenced within many WordPress templates, and many web pages in general to create movement, to allow for dynamically functioning elements in a more robust way than simple CSS and HTML animations and transitions.

If you haven't yet, you might want to set up a basic HTML page in your code editor, (I prefer Sublime Text) and try out a couple of things to get started. For the sake of simplicity, let's start by adding a red heading and a blue paragraph.

 How to create a basic HTML document:

```
1
2    <!DOCTYPE html>
3      <head>
4        <style>
5        h1 {color: red}
6        p {color: blue;}
7
8        </style>
9      </head>
10   <html>
11     <body>
12       <h1>My First Heading</h1>
13       <p>My first paragraph.</p>
14     </body>
15   </html>
16
```

 How to create a basic HTML document that has two boxes with images and text in them.

So add that to your document, and then view the document in a browser, to see your first bit of code come to life. Try entering this below into your document, and you can see you'll have two blocks, each with a placeholder image and text in them.

```
1
2    <!DOCTYPE html>
3    <html>
4        <head>
5            <style>
6            h1 {color: red}
7            p {color: blue;}
8            .boxy {display: inline-block; width: 44%; margin: 1%; padding: 2%; float: left;}
9            .lefty {background-color: #efefef;}
10           .righty {background-color: #efefef;}
11           .boxy img {width: 100%;}
12           </style>
13       </head>
14       <body>
15           <h1>My First Heading</h1>
16           <div class="lefty boxy">
17               <img src="https://lorempixel.com/g/400/200/">
18               <p>This is my left div</p>
19           </div>
20           <div class="righty boxy">
21               <img src="https://lorempixel.com/g/400/200/">
22               <p>This is my right div</p>
23           </div>
24       </body>
25   </html>
26
```

And that should look something like this when you load it in a browser:

My First Heading

This is my left div

This is my right div

With the process of experimentation and extensive Googling, you'll find more ways to manipulate the items and code on the page. It's nice to take a basic design and try to duplicate it with code.

39

You'll want to keep practicing with these elements, coding some basic websites and familiarizing yourself with HTML and CSS further:

If you are not super familiar with these elements, it's important to try to create some (at least simple) web pages in this format before you're going to be able to progress much further in this course. Here are some basic templates you could try your hand with: Open Source Web Design. Perhaps by looking at the way these are put together you'll be able to improve. I found that the best way to test out my skills was to try to make a portfolio site to showcase my skills as soon as I was able. This put me up against challenges I wanted to implement and sometimes didn't know how.

 The more speed bumps you get over, the more you set yourself apart from your non-coding compadres, use the tension between you and what you don't know to drive you, and get excited at small victories:

This tension between what we know and don't know helps us grow only if only if we have the right attitude. That attitude means understanding it will be a journey, and we're only at the beginning. If we're committed to this, then the more 'speed bumps' in the learning of coding we get over, the more we set ourselves apart from those who can't code.

We expand our functional knowledge to be able to be more useful to people. When we are able to create a WordPress site that a client could edit easily without knowing code, the core value is that of helping businesses thrive. This excites me, and I hope it serves as stimulation to help drive you further into learning this valuable skill that you can use to help create value for your clients as they serve their customers and make a living, but you can also use to make a living for yourself.

Don't be shy of PHP. Here are some sure-fire ways to adventure safely on the high seas of WordPress loops and the key concepts of starting with WordPress PHP. Here are examples of how you might use this.

 The key elements of WordPress PHP and how to kickstart your work with WordPress templates:

Perhaps you've familiarized yourself with HTML and CSS, and you're simply looking to get on board with WordPress and WordPress PHP. Some key elements of WordPress PHP you'll want to familiarize yourself with are:

The main loop: this brings in the content from the post or page and into the template. You can have 10 pages use the same template structure, for instance, and only the content would change out.

```
1
2    <?php the_content() ?>
3
```

On a page or post template you'd likely want to get the header with this code snippet:

```
1
2    <?php get_header(); ?>
3
```

Also, to get the footer, you could use this snippet:

```
1
2    <?php get_footer(); ?>
3
```

To get the default sidebar (anything you put into sidebar.php) use this:

```
1
2    <?php get_sidebar(); ?>
3
```

This is an example of calling the blog name within a "Heading 1" tag (H1):

```
1
2    <h1><?php bloginfo('name'); ?></h1>
3
```

One of the best things about WordPress is its friendliness with article-type sites or blogs. This is how you'd display a list of posts on an index page like index.php. As you can see here, there is a bit of HTML mixed into the PHP to provide a little structure around each post.

```
1
2    <?php if(have_posts()) : while(have_posts()) : the_post(); ?>
3      <h2><?php the_title(); ?></h2>
4      <?php the_content(); ?>
5    <?php endif(); ?>
6
```

If you want to display a list of posts on a non-index page (like page. php or home-page.php) you'd use a more custom loop, such as the one below. Here each post is in a <li> tag, or List Item. You can change the HTML and the PHP will still function the same as long as it stays intact.

```
 1
 2   <ul>
 3     <?php
 4     global $post;
 5     $args = array( 'posts_per_page' => 5, 'offset'=> 1, 'category' => 1 );
 6     $myposts = get_posts( $args );
 7     foreach ( $myposts as $post ) :
 8       setup_postdata( $post ); ?>
 9       <li>
10         <a href="<?php the_permalink(); ?>">
11           <?php the_title(); ?>
12         </a>
13       </li>
14     <?php endforeach;
15     wp_reset_postdata(); ?>
16   </ul>
17
```

This is a very basic listing to get you started. We'll talk through further application of this type of loop once we discuss a basic application. So now that we have PHP and HTML, all that we would need is to add some CSS to style the <li> and the post. Although we were putting CSS in the header for the experimentation above, we'd want to add this CSS to the stylesheet, either style.css or another stylesheet you've defined in your header, or more ideally in your functions.php file.

If you want to use your template for the front page, but only show a couple things differently, you could wrap them in this PHP below, and if under "Settings > Reading" the page is selected, and it is your "home" page, you'll see the items wrapped in the loop.

```
 1
 2   <?php if(is_front_page()) : ?>
 3     Do something if this is the front page...
 4   <?php endif; ?>
 5
```

Often you'll want to create a unique page for unique structure. Remember you'll add this to the header of the template:

```php
1
2  <?php
3    /*
4    Template Name: City Landing Page Template
5    */
6  ?>
7
```

In the page editor you'll select the page template. Select it from the template dropdown as shown below, and press "Update."

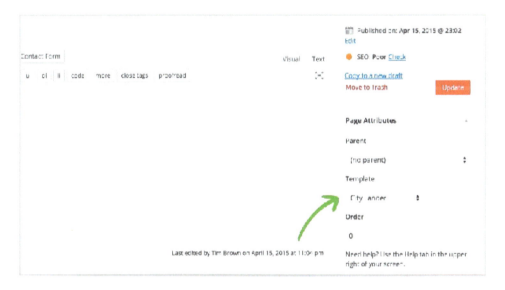

You can also make a change in a template only for a specific page by wrapping it in the loop below.

```php
1
2  <?php if(is_page('about')) :?>
3    Do something on the about page...
4  <?php endif; ?>
5
```

CHAPTER FIVE

CREATING YOUR FIRST WORDPRESS THEME
FROM SCRATCH

Can't I just use a theme? What are the benefits of creating a WordPress site from scratch?

One of the biggest problems with just using a theme is that you think of the problem in terms of what the theme lets you do instead of what's best for the client or the website, or what's best to help the visitors do what they want or you want them to do.

I started making websites for clients by modifying themes. I tried not to be hemmed in by the theme, but in the end, if there's a theme option that's 80% as good as what I had intended, I'd use it, because hey, who wouldn't? The idea of creating a theme from scratch to match the visual design that you made where you didn't even have a theme in mind means that you can design with the client and their customer in mind instead of designing from some one-size-fits-all template.

By creating a site from scratch around a visual design that's intended to serve the client and their customer's needs rather than fit a pre-built template, you're setting your services up as a custom high-value solution rather than a run-of-the-mill commodity.

If all you do is implement content and a couple tweaks within something that already existed, you may not be able to share your hard work as the custom high-end solution that you are trying to sell your work as. I find developing from scratch (I usually use a responsive naked framework as a starting point) reminds me to relentlessly seek the best solution, not the easiest.

What are some basic "naked" theme frameworks I can use to start off right in WordPress development?

_TK is a solid naked theme based on bootstrap (a CSS framework for responsive design structure) and Underscores (the maker's of WordPress' naked theme with the PHP loops set up) to get get started on.

With Bootstrap's out-of-the-gate responsive design features, mobile menu, and many bits and pieces of functionality like dropdowns, show/hides, and some basic styles built in, you have a tool that gets projects up off the ground quickly but doesn't impose too intense of initial style on your project.

With _Underscores pleasant start-up kit of your basic PHP loops you can get into theming without having all this stuff memorized or consulting WordPress documentation for every tiny thing.

Combine them together and you have _tk. I have been on a project using this framework and it did its job beautifully. WordPress developers would do well to become acquainted with this base theme for the obvious reasons. It has a quick start time on projects and, of course, the loose restrictions that a very basic theme will give you. Of course by knowing this, it's important to note you will have to write a good amount of CSS overlaying on what bootstrap's styles are. It would be a very boring site indeed that used out-of-the-box styles without modification to create a compelling design. Get the _tk Starter Theme Here.

This is, in the end, why someone would want to use a tool like this. The very basic styling that comes with Bootstrap is intended to be helpful without being obtrusive, and enables developers and designers to bring their own flare to the table and adjust things without being overly designed to begin with.

Here's how you get started writing your theme from scratch, and the main things you'll need to have in place for it to work

 With a new theme, the key things to have in place first is a Style.css file with the name of the theme up at the top, a page.php, header.php, and footer.php files with proper PHP loops.

 An example of a CSS file for WordPress, which will define the theme:

In chapter two, I showed you how to do this for a child theme, but the header of your CSS file for the parent theme should look like this, and if the file has to be named 'style.css' and be in the root folder of the theme.

```
1   /*
2   Theme Name:      Theme Name
3   Theme URI:       https://www.timbdesign.com/theme-page
4   Description:     The theme for "Theme Name"
5   Author:          Tim B Design
6   Author URI:      https://www.timbdesign.com
7   Template:        theme_name
8   Version:         1.0.0
9   */
10
11
12  /* ----------All your styles can be below here ---------------- */
```

Here is some code that you might use as a very basic header:

It first defines the doctype, displays the title for browsers to read using a WordPress PHP loop, and gets the favicon for the site if you have it dropped in the theme folder. The "body class" is applied to the tag so that page templates and ID's are automatically added for easy targeting with CSS classes. Clearly a basic header structure is included here, and the menu is called, so that whatever menu you are referring to in the WordPress admin as the "primary" will show up in the admin bar. Of course, if you are working in a blank theme, none of this will be styled yet, but it will just be raw elements that you can get ready to shape once we have the bones in place.

```php
1   /**
2    * The Header for our theme.
3    *
4    * Displays all of the <head> section, header and top navigation areas
5    *
6    * @package theme_name
7    *
8    */
9   ?><!DOCTYPE html>
10  <html <?php language_attributes(); ?>>
11      <head>
12      <meta charset="<?php bloginfo( 'charset' ); ?>" />
13      <title><?php wp_title(); ?></title>
14      <link rel="profile" href="http://gmpg.org/xfn/11" />
15      <link rel="pingback" href="<?php bloginfo( 'pingback_url' ); ?>" />
16      <link rel="shortcut icon" href="<?php echo get_template_directory_uri(); ?>/favicon.ico" />
17
18  <?php wp_head(); ?>
19  </head>
20  <body <?php body_class(); ?>>
21
22  <div id="wrap">
23
24      <header id="branding">
25          <div id="logo"><a href="<?php echo home_url() ?>/"><?php bloginfo( 'name' ); ?></a></div>
26          <div id="tagline"><?php bloginfo( 'description' ); ?></div>
27      </header>
28
29      <nav id="top-nav">
30          <?php wp_nav_menu( array( 'container_class' => 'menu-header', 'theme_location' => 'primary' ) ); ?>
31      </nav>
```

 Here is some code that you might use as a very basic footer:

Included is a simple footer with the current year, a copyright, and the end tags for the page. The <?php wp_footer(); ?> is needed to recognize this file as the footer and is used as well to call in files like some JavaScript files and so on when we add those via the functions.php file.

```
1    <?php
2    /**
3     * The template for displaying the footer.
4     *
5     * @package theme_name
6     */
7    ?>
8        <footer>
9            <p>&copy; <?php echo date( 'Y' ); ?> <?php bloginfo( 'name' ); ?></p>
10       </footer>
11
12   </div><!-- end of wrapper -->
13   <?php wp_footer(); ?>
14   </body>
15   </html>
```

Of course, if you've downloaded one of the starter themes above you'll already have these things in place, plus some divs and structure that will be used for quickly shaping the responsive aspects of the site.

In the next chapter, I will share how to get some basic responsive structure in place if you are working from complete scratch, and how to start manipulating the design if you are using a responsive framework, like one of those above.

CHAPTER SIX

WORKING WITH
RESPONSIVE DESIGN

 Modifying a theme, retaining current responsive design, and implementing responsive on a current theme

So, you're likely very aware that responsive design is the art of making a website's content conform and re-arrange based on the size of the screen so that a visitor can interact with the website more easily. At one point in the history of our beloved smartphones, even Apple expected us to tap on a section of the screen and zoom into regular websites. Little did we know that responsive design would change the way we look at content on the web and add an extra element into our workflow as designers and developers.

 Don't rewrite the guidebook if you have a theme with responsive qualities – look at the conventions it's using and use those to leverage already written code to conform divs and display responsively:

Most modern WordPress themes have some responsive conventions baked in already. If you were to rewrite them with your own media queries, you would be using redundant code or code that is written for the purpose of solving a problem that was already solved previously.

 Here's an example of leveraging the themes responsive design – for a theme called 'Bridge.'

The bridge theme is a solid and versatile theme that you can get off of Themeforest. Let's say I wanted to create a template that has custom elements in it, and whole new pieces of functionality, but not write redundant code around the responsive aspects of the theme. I take a look at how the theme is creating the divs for four columns that stack on top of each other in mobile, like so. (Right click, inspect element.)

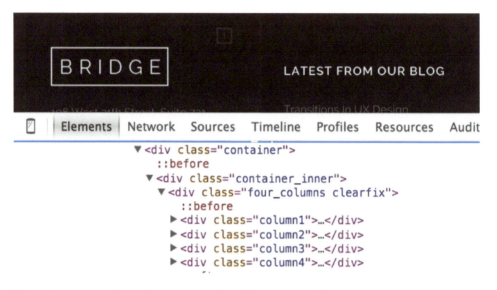

Now I can see that they are using the convention:

```
 1 ▼ <div class="container">
 2      <div class="container_inner">
 3      <div class="four_columns clearfix">
 4      <div class="column1">
 5      <div class="column_inner">
 6      </div>
 7      </div>
 8      <div class="column2">
 9      <div class="column_inner">
10      </div>
11      </div>
12      <div class="column3">
13      <div class="column_inner">
14      </div>
15      </div>
16      <div class="column4">
17      <div class="column_inner">
18      </div>
19      </div>
20      </div>
21      </div>
22      </div>
```

Instead of making my own four-column grid, it's advised that I use what's already built for the above mentioned reasons. In this case, three columns and two columns also will work. Of course, the CSS is written for these, and each theme will likely have some different conventions. The point is to look and see what they are using and unless it was poorly done, use their conventions.

Working with Bootstrap, Foundation, or another framework for responsive with a WordPress theme

Using Bootstrap within your theme:

Bootstrap is lovely, and is baked into a lot of free and commercial themes out there, including the _tk starter theme that I'm suggesting people use to get started. To use the responsive elements of Bootstrap within your theme, it's a matter of working around PHP loops and using the conventions you can use off of Bootstrap's website.

```
1   <div class="container">
2       <div class="jumbotron">
3           <h1>My First Bootstrap Page</h1>
4           <p>Resize this responsive page to see the effect!</p>
5       </div>
6       <div class="row">
7           <div class="col-sm-4">
8               <h3>Column 1</h3>
9               <p>Lorem ipsum dolor sit amet, consectetur adipisicing elit...</p>
10              <p>Ut enim ad minim veniam, quis nostrud exercitation ullamco laboris...</p>
11          </div>
12          <div class="col-sm-4">
13              <h3>Column 2</h3>
14              <p>Lorem ipsum dolor sit amet, consectetur adipisicing elit...</p>
15              <p>Ut enim ad minim veniam, quis nostrud exercitation ullamco laboris...</p>
16          </div>
17          <div class="col-sm-4">
18              <h3>Column 3</h3>
19              <p>Lorem ipsum dolor sit amet, consectetur adipisicing elit...</p>
20              <p>Ut enim ad minim veniam, quis nostrud exercitation ullamco laboris...</p>
21          </div>
22      </div>
23  </div>
```

So to use on a page where you want to include the sidebar in one-fourth column to the right you'd use this format in the main container for the page:

```
1   <div class="container">
2   <div class="row">
3   <div class="col-md-8">
4   <div id="primary" class="content-area">
5   <main id="main" class="site-main" role="main">
6
7   <?php while ( have_posts() ) : the_post(); ?>
```

```
1     <?php the_title(''); ?>
```

```
1    <?php the_content(''); ?><?php endwhile; // end of the loop. ?>
2
3    </main><!-- #main -->
4    </div><!-- #primary -->
5    </div>
6    <div class="col-md-4">
7    <?php get_sidebar(); ?>
8    </div>
9    </div>
10   </div>
```

This is just a basic page where "the_content" piece pulls from the page editor as long as you name the template page.php. For any WordPress site, you can add a piece at the top of the page template that delineates the template as an alternative template and allows you to choose it in the page editor when you're adding content to apply the template.

For instance, this is how it looks if I name template "Right Sidebar":

```
1
2   <?php
3   /*
4   Template Name: Right Sidebar
5   *
6   *
7   */
8
9   get_header(); ?>
```

Using Foundation within your theme:

Foundation is a great framework with what some might consider classier visual design assets right out of the box. To me this isn't necessarily the biggest selling point, because although I appreciate its flat design, I usually change the look of this framework's elements to match a desired visual design rather than use any look they have out of the box. That said, this is another great option for creating responsive sites without writing the responsive base from scratch.

The PHP could remain the same, but if you used Zurb's Foundation for your responsive framework, the same page template would look like this in its entirety:

54

```php
1   <?php
2   /*
3   Template Name: Right Sidebar with Foundation
4   *
5   *
6   */
7
8   get_header(); ?>
9
10  <div class="row">
11
12
13    <div class="large-9 columns">
14    <div id="primary" class="content-area">
15    <main id="main" class="site-main" role="main">
16
17
18    <?php while ( have_posts() ) : the_post(); ?>
19
20    <?php the_title() ?>
21
22    <?php the_content() ?>
23
24    <?php endwhile; // end of the loop. ?>
25    </main><!-- #main -->
26    </div><!-- #primary -->
27    </div>
28
29
30    <div class="large-3 columns">
31    <?php get_sidebar(); ?>
32    </div>
33  </div>
34
35
36  <?php get_footer(); ?>
```

 Other solid responsive frameworks and how to use them in your theme:

Skeleton: When you don't need all the extra stuff, just the responsive grid.

Gumby Framework: Another solid option. Although it's officially retired, its base is still good and Gumby Framework includes templates and a UI Kit for your designers.

HTML 5 Bones: Another lightweight responsive framework. Nothing but the HTML essentials.

Kube: Back to the ones with a nice mobile menu built in. Kube touts beautiful out-of-the-box typography and use of modern flexbox.

Developing a responsive WordPress site without a framework

Oh, you fancy devil, you! You don't want a framework at all. You want to bake a pie like mama did and ground your own flour. Have no fear. Those new to HTML and CSS should be aware that the core responsive elements of most of these frameworks are pretty goll-darn simple when it comes down to it. I'll start you down the road to learning how to set up your responsive framework here.

 Basic media queries for common devices:

Probably the most insightful thing I read about this came from Ralph M. in a 'Stack Overflow' comment:

"Rather than try to target @media rules at specific devices, it is arguably more practical to base them on your particular layout instead. That is, gradually narrow your desktop browser window and observe the natural breakpoints for your content. It's different for every site. As long as the design flows well at each browser width, it should work pretty reliably on any screen size (and there are lots and lots of them out there.)"

For this I use a Chrome plugin "Window Resizer" to give me the sizes at which my design needs a media query for. Here are some examples of common media queries in 2015 to help kickstart your journey toward designing in the browser. Enjoy!

```
1   /* Extra small devices (phones, 320px and up) */
2   @media (min-width: 320px) { ... }
3
4   /* Small devices (tablets, 768px and up) */
5   @media (min-width: 768px) { ... }
6
7   /* Medium devices (desktops, 992px and up) */
8   @media (min-width: 992px) { ... }
9
10  /* Large devices (large desktops, 1200px and up) */
11  @media (min-width: 1200px) { ... }
```

Working with mobile menus in WordPress without using a responsive framework:

This would be another chapter entirely, but for a mobile menu you can write one from HTML, CSS and Jquery if you so desire. Here is a tutorial on that from Inspirational Pixels.

 Quick cheat for a mobile menu on the fly in WordPress (Plugins)

Responsive Menu Plugin
WP Responsive Menu

Both well-reviewed, although I can only vouch for the second one, as I used it and it was pretty great with a lot of customizable options.

CHAPTER SEVEN

CREATING CUSTOM POST TYPES AND TAXONOMIES
IN WORDPRESS

What are custom post types and taxonomies and how can we use them to create great websites for ourselves and clients?

WordPress is powerful partly because of its ability to use custom post types, categories and taxonomies. For instance if I need a portfolio custom post type, I can set one up in WordPress, give a separate template and also make a listing that will list out all of the items within that post type that I 'ask it to.' For instance, archive-portfolio.php and I can make a custom template to showcase a single portfolio item at single-portfolio.php. You can also use the WordPress loop on any template with a custom query, but these are items we'll cover in the next chapter. For now, we'll show you how to get started setting up these custom post types and 'taxonomies.' Taxonomies, like categories or tags, are simply ways to organize your content.

 The value of custom post types and leveraging them in your WordPress websites

You can have custom post types for everything. Symptoms or treatments for hospitals, slider items, team members, and any kind of directory or listing you'd like to display in a unique or easy way that allows yourself or a client to easily add to. When setting up a new custom post type you can see it as an icon and title in the sidebar of your WordPress Admin. This makes things clean and easy for someone editing their WordPress site. As sites get more complicated, custom post types become more important.

The value of custom taxonomies and leveraging them in your WordPress websites

Custom taxonomies are nice ways to organize your content. You could use categories and tags to organize everything because they are easy to add to your custom post types, but I like taxonomies because I can show them underneath a custom post type as essentially a category of categories. For example, I had a client that wanted to be able to add mugs, and as they entered them they could choose shape, glaze color, and handle type easily from the admin because of custom taxonomies. Also with these 'categories of categories' I could allow people to search and filter through them with each taxonomy having its own filtering dropdown.

 How to set up a custom post type with and without a plugin

I suggest getting started by learning how to define custom post types without installing a plugin to handle them because they're fairly easy to do – but I'm not saying you have to do it that way every time. Many people like to have as much control over structural elements like this as possible, which means defining them manually so someone else's plugin doesn't unnecessarily hold all the control over their site.

Working with Custom Post Types: the Plugin Route

Know that disabling a custom post type plugin like the one I'm about to suggest will essentially disable your site if it is using custom post types in critical areas. Renaming your custom post type will lose the association with your content as well. I'm addressing concerns here that reviewers have brought up in reviewing Custom Post Type UI.

The main drawbacks seem to be things that would be true if you had written your Custom Post Type separate from this plugin as well. Try this plugin, however, and read the reviews, it's called Custom Post Type UI. Here's a screenshot of adding a new custom post type:

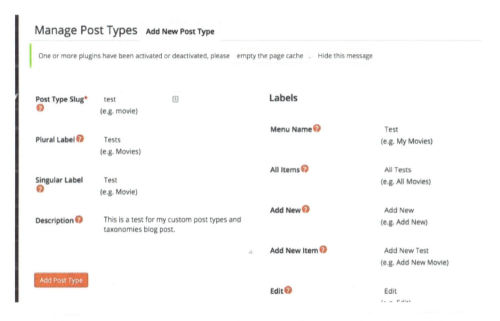

I found the interface easy enough to use. Essentially when adding new custom post types it takes some time to define all the items, and you'll have to do that no matter if you use a plugin or the code snippets below. Adding via this plugin is your choice, just make an informed decision.

 ## Working with custom post types without someone else's plugin – with code snippets

I personally add my custom post types as a custom written plugin, so that it's separate from the site's theme. The idea is to make sure your content and structure can live happily on their own. For instance, if you changed themes, then all of your portfolio items of symptoms for a medical site wouldn't be lost with your theme.

So to add a new custom post type you need to define its title, singular and plural uses, if it will be hierarchical, if you want to have a custom dash icon, and a couple other things, and you're good to go. Here's an example of one. To activate this, save it as plugin-name. php, zip it up and upload it to your site as a plugin. Then activate it.

```php
<?php
/*
Plugin Name: Portfolio Items
Plugin URI: https://timbdesign.com/
Description: Declares a plugin that will create a custom post type displaying portfolio items.
Version: 1.0
Author: Tim Brown
Author URI: https://timbdesign.com/
License: GPLv2
*/
?>

// Creates Portfolio Items Custom Post Type
function portfolio_items_init() {
	$args = array(
	'label' => 'Portfolio Items',
	'public' => true,
	'show_ui' => true,
	'capability_type' => 'post',
	'hierarchical' => false,
	'rewrite' => array('slug' => 'portfolio-items'),
	'query_var' => true,
	'menu_icon' => 'dashicons-desktop',
	'supports' => array(
	'title',
	'editor',
	'excerpt',
	'trackbacks',
	'custom-fields',
	'comments',
	'revisions',
	'thumbnail',
	'author',
	'page-attributes',)
	);
	register_post_type( 'portfolio-items', $args );
}
add_action( 'init', 'portfolio_items_init' );
```

You can also swap out all of these items with what you're needing in a custom post type. A couple things to make sure of are to make the function at the beginning and init / action at the end both the same, and only use underscores, not dashes in these spots.

If you want to easily generate these things you can use Custom Post Type Generator by Thememergency.

How to set up a custom taxonomy with and without a plugin

Custom Taxonomies: The plugin Route

The same plugin above can allow you to quickly execute custom taxonomies. Custom Post Type UI is great for this, and I might start using it in the future just because of the speed it allows for in creating these.

Custom taxonomies without a plugin

Once again when I say without a plugin, I'm actually suggesting you essentially place this in your own simple plugin, containing any Custom Post Types and taxonomies. In this situation we'd add this to the same plugin that we created above, and these topics would apply to whatever post type you enter where this snippet below says 'portfolio-items.'

```
1   //hook into the init action and call create_topics_nonhierarchical_taxonomy when it fires
2
3   add_action( 'init', 'create_topics_nonhierarchical_taxonomy', 0 );
4
5   function create_topics_nonhierarchical_taxonomy() {
6
7   // Labels part for the GUI
8
9     $labels = array(
10      'name' => _x( 'Topics', 'taxonomy general name' ),
11      'singular_name' => _x( 'Topic', 'taxonomy singular name' ),
12      'search_items' => __( 'Search Topics' ),
13      'popular_items' => __( 'Popular Topics' ),
14      'all_items' => __( 'All Topics' ),
15      'parent_item' => null,
16      'parent_item_colon' => null,
17      'edit_item' => __( 'Edit Topic' ),
18      'update_item' => __( 'Update Topic' ),
19      'add_new_item' => __( 'Add New Topic' ),
20      'new_item_name' => __( 'New Topic Name' ),
21      'separate_items_with_commas' => __( 'Separate topics with commas' ),
22      'add_or_remove_items' => __( 'Add or remove topics' ),
23      'choose_from_most_used' => __( 'Choose from the most used topics' ),
24      'menu_name' => __( 'Topics' ),
25    );
26
27  // Now register the non-hierarchical taxonomy like tag
28
29    register_taxonomy('topics','portfolio-items',array(
30      'hierarchical' => false,
31      'labels' => $labels,
32      'show_ui' => true,
33      'show_admin_column' => true,
34      'update_count_callback' => '_update_post_term_count',
35      'query_var' => true,
36      'rewrite' => array( 'slug' => 'topic' ),
37    ));
38  }
```

f you want to generate this and not change out everything in this snippet, you can use GenerateWP's easy-to-use Custom Taxonomy Generator.

 Getting the Most out of Custom Taxonomies: Some Final Notes.

Always think through the categories and sub-categories before creating this whole infrastructure. I use this particularly for things I want to sort or show based on different attributes. I make sure I know the key categories and sub-categories for the items based on the client's needs. Then, and only then, do I create custom post types and taxonomies. Otherwise content might need to be re-added if I have to change them later.

CHAPTER EIGHT

UTILIZING THE WORDPRESS LOOP TO DISPLAY POSTS IN

ARCHIVES AND PAGES

How the WordPress loop works and why it makes WordPress awesome.

WordPress is special in its ability to loop through posts and in this way you can style the blog loop one time and it works for all of the posts. I find this an incredible asset for easy development once one gets a decent understanding of it, and I think you will, too. WordPress was once a meager blogging platform, but in this day and age of content-heavy websites, the core of its functions, such as 'the loop', really shine and allow people to showcase their site's content whether it be blog articles, locations, symptoms, doctors or products. Anything that can be categorized and sorted and that you want to show in a unique way, you can use the WordPress loop for.

 Setting up the Loop:

What we'll be doing here is just communicating with the database via PHP, and saying if you have posts. Display them while you got 'em. Show the title, the thumbnail image for the post, and a little bit of the post so people can see what it's about. If there aren't posts yet, tell the visitor that.

All you need to start with the loop is this simple snippet:

```php
<?php if ( have_posts() ) : while ( have_posts() ) : the_post(); ?>

    <h2><?php the_title() ;?></h2>
    <?php the_post_thumbnail(); ?>
    <?php the_excerpt(); ?>

<?php endwhile; else: ?>

    <p>Sorry, no posts to list</p>

<?php endif; ?>
```

Don't let me over-complicate it for you, just get started using the loop on your site now. Experiment with it and start getting your hands dirty, because no amount of reading will fully prepare you. You have to have real things you want to do, and you will come up against roadblocks and look for solutions. Google and Stack Overflow are your best friends while developing.

 Examples of formatting in an archive loop:

Now you can implement some HTML with your loop. You just always want to start and end your PHP before adding the HTML. at the end. Other than that, you can just use your standard HTML and CSS classes. Here's a nice simple example of incorporating in some HTML. Feel free to copy it into your site or just learn from the principles demonstrated here.

```
1   <div class="posts-wrapper">
2   <?php if ( have_posts() ) : while ( have_posts() ) : the_post(); ?>
3
4   <article id="post-<?php the_ID(); ?>" <?php if(is_category('featured')): ?>class="featured-post"<?php endif; ?>>
5       <h1 class="post-title"><?php the_title() ;?></h1>
6
7       <p class="date-and-category">
8           Published on <?php the_time('M j, Y'); ?>
9           by <?php the_category(', '); ?>
10          in <?php the_category(', '); ?>
11      </p>
12
13      <div class="post-content"><?php the_content(); ?></div>
14
15      <div class="prev-next-links">
16          <ul>
17              <li class="next-post"><?php next_post_link(); ?></li>
18              <li class="prev-post"><?php previous_post_link(); ?></li>
19          </ul>
20
21      </div>
22
23  </article>
24
25  <?php endwhile; else: ?>
26
27      <p>Sorry, this post does not exist</p>
28
29  <?php endif; ?>
30  </div>
```

As you can see, I'm simply adding some basic HTML with CSS classes to elements so I can style them in my CSS file.

 Some last considerations

How to use the WordPress loop to display posts in pages or other places in your WordPress site

Why you would want to do this:

What if you want a listing of posts in your footer? Or want to use posts in your sidebar? You don't have to use a plugin for bits and pieces like this! Just drop a loop like the one below into your template.

Setting up your loop:

```php
<?php

    $args = array(
        'orderby' => 'title',
        'post_type' => 'cpt-name'
    );
    $the_query = new WP_Query( $args );

?>

<?php if ( $the_query->have_posts() ) : while ( $the_query->have_posts() ) : $the_query->the_post(); ?>

    <h1 class="the-title"><?php the_title() ;?></h1>
    <div class="post-excerpt"><?php the_excerpt(); ?></div>

<?php endwhile; else: ?>

    <p>Sorry, there are no posts to display</p>

<?php endif; ?>
```

If you are using more than one loop per page, you'll want to clear out each loop with this sweet little nugget of glory.

```php
<?php wp_reset_query(); ?>
```

You just need to drop it in-between loops, so the database query knows to reset, and it makes it possible to list another grouping of posts with no problems.

CHAPTER NINE

USING ADVANCED CUSTOM FIELDS TO SUPERCHARGE
WORDPRESS EDITABILITY

Why and when to use advanced custom fields to create highly editable sites

You may have tried to edit a WordPress website five years ago and found it difficult or cumbersome, and if you had, you might not have realized why. The truth is that WordPress out of the box allows for templates and then a big "Wysiwyg" or "What you see is what you get" editor, but that text area/editor inserts all of the content a web admin enters all in one spot within the template. So the backend template can only show all of that content in one spot, and if you try to put structure within the "Wysiwyg" editor it makes it very easy for something to get broken. Enter "Advanced Custom Fields." Advanced Custom Fields allow you to give fields to a WordPress admin user and inject the photos or text they enter in those fields super easily wherever you want them into the template. It's actually incredible, and it makes it way more easy to give clients a website they can have a lot more control over, and create a site that's not dependent on one big text area, but rather, it uses many bits of content. This is crucial for a better experience for site visitors.

So now you know why. Here's when to use ACF's in your template:

Here's a quick example of ACFs (how I'll refer to Advanced Custom Fields for the rest of the article) in action within the template so you can calm down about how hard this is going to be:

```
1    <?php the_field('field_name'); ?>
```

And creating the fields – of many types – is all done within the WordPress admin, and you add them conditionally to certain page and post types as you need them.

 Some example use cases of ACF in a site:

You can use ACF's for almost anything in a WordPress site, but let me give you some quick examples. You can use them for an image on the home page and place it exactly where you want within your code structure/template, text areas, color pickers for backgrounds and background images, and you can use them as a "repeater" or flexible content field. This will give the people adding and editing content to the WordPress site as much or as little control over the site as will make sense for them.

 How to create the fields within the WordPress admin and associating them with templates

 suggest getting started by learning how to define custom post types without installing a plugin to handle them because they're fairly easy to do – but I'm not saying you have to do it that way every time. Many people like to have as much control over structural elements like this as possible, which means defining them manually so someone else's plugin doesn't hold all the control over their site unnecessarily.

 Install the WordPress Advanced Custom Field's plugin:

You can find the basic (still highly functional) version of Advanced Custom Fields here.

bit.ly/advancedcf

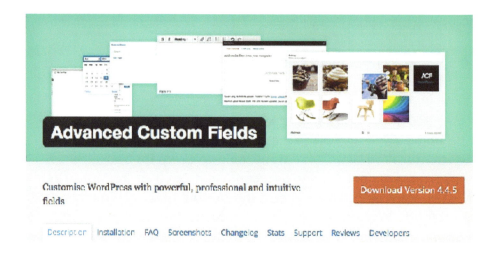

Advanced Custom Fields

Customise WordPress with powerful, professional and intuitive fields

Download Version 4.4.5

Description | Installation FAQ Screenshots Changelog Stats Support Reviews Developers

If you are going to be developing any sites that could really use a lot of edibility from the people that would be adding and updating content on a regular basis, I'd suggest getting the premium version – Advanced Custom Fields Pro. It really depends on what you need though. Because the fields will transfer over to Pro if you ever have to switch, I might consider waiting until you need a feature of Pro and buying it then. The repeater field, gallery field, flexible content fields and options pages are all elements of Pro that I'd rather not do without as they are glorious.

So anyways, download and install or go to Plugins > "Add New" in the WordPress admin to get the free version of Advanced Custom Fields, press "Install Now" and activate ACF.

 Add the fields you want to give to the WordPress admin user to easily edit:

Once you have the plugin installed and activated, go to "Custom Fields" on the right menu in the WordPress admin and "Add New" field group. Once you have a new group added, you can start adding the types of fields you'll want to make easy for the people who will be adding content to the site. For instance, in the picture below I'm adding an image field called "Mobile Screenshot."

Now for simple images you'll want to make sure "Image URL" is selected unless you want to use the more complicated ACF loop, which allows for alt text, etc.

 Add the The Advanced Custom Field to your template:

The usage for this simple way of adding an image with image URL looks like this in the template:

```
1    <img src="<?php the_field('mobile_screenshot') ?>" alt="Mobile Screenshot for Portfolio Project" />
```

You can also use the full image with the preferred alt text by choosing "Image Array" from the ACF menu, then add the image to the template this way:

```
1   <?php
2
3   $image = get_field('mobile_screenshot');
4
5   if( !empty($image) ): ?>
6
7       <img src="<?php keyword">echo $image['url']; ?>" alt="<?php echo $image['alt']; ?>" />
8
9   <?php endif; ?>
```

How to add advanced custom fields to WordPress templates, with five more examples

Just to clarify, each of these fields needs to placed among other code within the template you are editing. It can be within the loop on a post listing page, or a custom post type listing page, on your home, about or contact page, or any type of page or post content. You just need to make sure that you choose to allow this type of Advanced Custom Field on that page, so admins can see them and choose what they want. Here's where you choose what pages or post they show up on:

The Basic Field in a couple different scenarios:

As long as you have your ACF settings allowing the field for that page or post type, you can add it to the template of that page or post type in a basic way like so:

```
1   <p class"yeah-buddy"><?php the_field('my_first_field') ?></p>
```

In this scenario, we'd have a Text field on the backend with a label of "My First Field," and a name of my_first_field. We just have to match what's in this code snippet with the name. We can wrap it in whatever divs and p-tags and whatever else we want to. This is where if you know HTML and CSS already, you should rejoice, as you should be seeing how much freedom this can give you for providing highly editable sites to your clients and people editing the sites. But if you're not yet, let's dive into some more epic applications of this amazing plugin.

 Adding a repeater field

To add a repeater field, you need to have ACF Pro (go buy it – one site is $25 or get unlimited for $100) and a repeater field will allow you to nest sub-fields within it. So let's say we want to have testimonials and we want there to be the copy for the testimonial, the author, and a link of the name to the author's website. We create this this way in the ACF plugin:

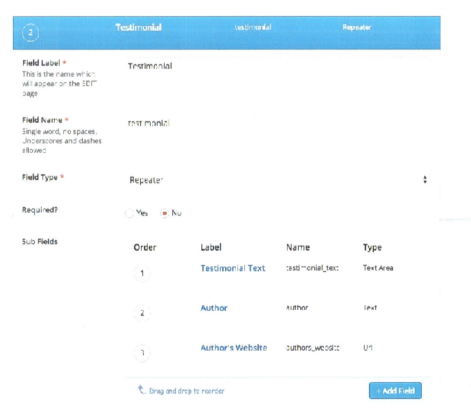

Then add it to the template like this (replace my HTML with whatever structure you want- included for reference):

```
1   <div class="testimonials-wrap">
2
3   <?php
4
5   // check if the repeater field has rows of data
6   if( have_rows('testimonial') ):
7
8       // loop through the rows of data
9       while ( have_rows('repeater_field_name') ) : the_row();
10  ?>
11  <div class="individual-testimonial-wrap">
12  <p text="testimonial-body"> <?php
13      // display a sub field value
14      the_sub_field('testimonial_text');
15  ?></p>
16
17  <a href="<?php the_sub_field('authors_website'); ?>"><?php the_sub_field('author') ?></a>
18  </div>
19  <?php
20      endwhile;
21
22  else :
23
24      // no rows found
25
26  endif;
27
28  ?>
29  </div>
```

 Showing a field or set of fields only if item is set in admin:

If you have some fields that the person entering content might not add, you can make them only show up if they have something entered like so.

```
1   <?php if( get_field('possible_field') ): ?>
2       <p>If it's added in the post: <?php the_field('possible_field'); ?></p>
3   <?php endif; ?>
```

 Getting the most of out Custom Taxonomies: some final notes:

There are so many more amazing ways to use Advanced Custom Fields in WordPress, this is only an introduction; however, I hope it was a useful one. If you're creating websites for clients, ACF can be one of the ways to make the website so much easier for them to use. After all, usability isn't just about the front-end user of a website.

CHAPTER TEN

THE WP LOOP WITH CUSTOM POST TYPES,
TAXONOMIES AND FIELDS

Examples of when you'd want to use custom post types, taxonomies and advanced custom fields together

The reason why I'm sharing examples of how to use these all together, is because I think if you can master using all of this stuff together, you'll be able to tackle just about anything WordPress can throw at you. **So consider this level's final boss.** If you can rock these things all together you are no longer a Noob. You can handle a ton of tasks in WordPress development, and are likely at least a Jr. Level WordPress Developer.

Using Custom Post Types, Taxonomies and Fields gives you freedom to make many kinds of websites

For example – Clinic

Custom Post Type: Doctor (Allows easy administration, adding and displaying a specific type of item)
Taxonomies: Specialties, Locations (Allows you to have categorization beyond stock categories to sort or display information)
Fields: Education, other "About" Information fields (Allows you to work these elements into styled templates without the client having to touch code)

Example – Book Publisher

Custom Post Type: Book (Allows publisher to add books easily in the sidebar of WordPress)
Taxonomies: Sort and Display the books by whatever categorization

structure you'd like.

Fields: Any extra information about the book, but that you don't need to use to sort as categories/taxonomies. The ISBN number, the description, so on and so forth.

 Brief refresher on where and how to set up custom post types, taxonomies, and advanced custom fields.

Custom Post Types can be set up through your WordPress theme's functions.php file, more preferably in a plugin of your own creation so they can be used even if you change themes, or you can also use a plugin like Pods or Custom Post Type UI. **Taxonomies** can be set up by any of these same means.

Once again, Advanced Custom Fields can be set up with a really awesome plugin here:

bit.ly/advancedcf

 A couple examples of loops using custom post types, taxonomies and advanced custom fields together

It's always best to learn from code snippets, and of course it's nice to be able to copy and paste. Here is a custom post type, taxonomies, and advanced custom fields working together in harmony from beginning to end (code). For instance this loop below is displaying books using a custom taxonomy "booktype" and only displaying items that have a booktype of "fiction."

As you can see, it would then display, each book with its title, ISBN number, a big introduction and then the content of the post. If there weren't any to display, it would give a little note about that. Then the query resets in case there are any other post listings on this page.

```php
1   <?php
2
3   $args = array(
4   'orderby' => 'title',
5   'post_type' => 'cpt-name-book',
6   'booktype' => 'fiction',
7   );
8   $the_query = new WP_Query( $args );
9
10  ?>
11
12  <?php if ( $the_query->have_posts() ) : while ( $the_query->have_posts() ) : $the_query->the_post(); ?>
13  <div class="each-book">
14  <h1 class="the-title"><?php the_title() ;?></h1>
15  <div class="isbn-number"><?php the_field('isbn_number'?></div>
16
17  <div class="big-intro"><?php the_field('book-introduction'?></div>
18  <div class="main-summary"><?php the_content() ?></div>
19  </div>
20
21  <?php endwhile; else: ?> <p>Sorry, there are no posts to display</p> <?php endif; ?>
22  <?php wp_reset_query(); ?>
```

 Of Course, if you wanted the above code to work, you would need to create the custom post type and taxonomy how you see fit and then add Advanced Custom Fields in the WordPress admin through the ACF plugin.

Review Chapter 7 for how to create custom post types and taxonomies, and Chapter 9 for how to create and add custom post types.

When wielded together, custom post types, taxonomies and ACF will allow you to use 'order' to "order" them in ascending or descending order.

```
1   'order' => 'ASC',
2
3   or
4
5   'order' => 'DESC',
```

'Order-by' allows you to sort by these 10 possible items (from WordPress Codex)

- 'none' – No order (available since Version 2.8)
- 'ID' – Order by post ID. Note the capitalization
- 'author' – Order by author
- 'title' – Order by title

- 'name' – Order by post name (post slug)
- 'type' – Order by post type (available since Version 4.0)
- 'date' – Order by date
- 'modified' – Order by last modified date
- 'parent' – Order by post/page parent ID
- 'rand' – Random order
- 'comment_count' – Order by number of comments (available since Version 2.9)
- 'menu_order' – Order by Page Order. Used most often for Pages (Order field in the Edit Page Attributes box) and for Attachments (the integer fields in the insert / upload media gallery dialog), but could be used for any post type with distinct 'menu_order' values (they all default to 0)
- 'meta_value' – Note that a 'meta_key=keyname' must also be present in the query. Note also that the sorting will be alphabetical, which is fine for strings (i.e. words), but can be unexpected for numbers (e.g. 1, 3, 34, 4, 56, 6, etc, rather than 1, 3, 4, 6, 34, 56 as you might naturally expect). Use 'meta_value_num' instead for numeric values. You may also specify 'meta_type' if you want to cast the meta value as a specific type. Possible values are 'NUMERIC', 'BINARY', 'CHAR', 'DATE', 'DATETIME', 'DECIMAL', 'SIGNED', 'TIME', 'UNSIGNED', same as in '$meta_query'. When using 'meta_type' you can also use meta_value_* accordingly. For example, when using DATETIME as 'meta_type' you can use 'meta_value_datetime' to define order structure
- 'meta_value_num' – Order by numeric meta value (available since Version 2.8). Also note that a 'meta_key=keyname' must also be present in the query. This value allows for numerical sorting as noted above in 'meta_value'
- 'post__in' – Preserve post ID order given in the post__in array (available since Version 3.5)

Here's one more example of a loop with a custom post type, a custom taxonomy, and advanced custom fields for medical:

```php
1   <?php
2
3       $args = array(
4       'orderby' => 'title',
5       'post_type' => 'doctor'
6       'specialty' => 'nose-and-throat',
7       );
8       $the_query = new WP_Query( $args );
9
10      ?>
11
12      <?php if ( $the_query->have_posts() ) : while ( $the_query->have_posts() ) : $the_query->the_post(); ?>
13      <div class="each-dr">
14      <h1 class="the-title"><?php the_title() ;?></h1>
15      <div class="isbn-number"><?php the_field('education'?></div>
16
17      <div class="big-intro"><?php the_field('about'?></div>
18      <div class="main-summary"><?php the_content() ?></div>
19      </div>
20
21      <?php endwhile; else: ?> <p>Sorry, there are no doctors to display.</p> <?php endif; ?>
22      <?php wp_reset_query(); ?>
```

 Utilize the power of all three of these components to create extensible WordPress websites that are as powerful as you need them. Start experimenting.

I hope you've been experimenting all along the way, but none of this knowledge will truly sink in until you put it to work. Let me offer encouragement, I've found learning how to use all three of these together has made my WordPress skills truly useful to many small businesses I've helped, my own portfolio, and now larger clients that I get to help as well.

 Your next steps:

There is more than one way to skin a cat, but if you've been able to follow along and implement this code, you have the basis for a strong way to create WordPress sites with any number of types of items, categorization and info without making the client touch any code. This is the beginning of greatness. Go forth and help clients!

CHAPTER ELEVEN

HOW TO PRICE YOURSELF APPROPRIATELY WHEN DOING
WORDPRESS DEVELOPMENT

 The 7% on marketing benchmark, and 35-50% of that for digital marketing

Pricing is an interesting beast no matter what industry you're in – WordPress development is no different. But I will attempt to clarify a few aspects for you. If you are in the U.S. market, there is still some variation for acceptable pricing and ranges within that for the sizes of projects / clients.

My overall approach to pricing is based on annual revenue that a business makes and what the website's value will be to them in the end.

Benchmarking suggests that companies spent 7% of their annual revenue on marketing, and 35% of that on digital marketing. This number is probably moving closer to half as time wears on.

 So for companies with 5 million dollars in revenue they might spend $350,000 on marketing:

This is for a given year. Understand that this is a benchmark, not a rule – so they could spend $0, if they are shrinking $150,000 total for the year, or if they are growing $500k.

The 35%-50% of this number allocated for digital marketing would be – $122,500 to $175,000.

I assume that a website on the year would be a significant amount of their digital marketing spend, but obviously couldn't eat the whole thing. So for the whole website I might expect a 5 Million dollar a year company to spend $42,875 on a website.

Another consideration that might drive down this number is that the website only brings in $200,000 on it's own per year and the rest is done through distributors, retail, or some other vehicle. Because the website does support those other efforts, but doesn't drive them, I would give the website 20% credit for other sales (being that it represents the company professionally and does help persuade them) = 1 Million dollars I'm valuing what this website can bring in / how much it's potentially able to help their business.

If it's done well it could literally increase sales 10 – 20% so $100k to $200k on the year. That's a big deal! But obviously they can't spend what they can expect in return on the site, or even half of it. There's a lot of overhead to running a business – tax, etc. But let's base our percentages off the 1.2 million number (sales attributed to being helped by or made from the website.)

 $84,000 x .35 = $29,400 = digital marketing spend on the website total over this next year

So in a smart business like that, that might be 14k in a build and 1.5 a month in SEO spend over the next year.

The rest of that 84 could go to social, PPC, etc. etc. Anything not directly website related.

A 14k build wouldn't be much for an agency, but might be great for a freelancer or a smaller agency, with 60% going to the development phase.

So the brass tax = **$8,400 would be my dev budget** on a project like that if I was the marketing director for that company and I was working with an outside agency.

The clincher – you can break down 84K a million ways, and if the business was totally driven by online sales, the full $122,500 (benchmark 35% digital marketing budget of 7% of total revenue) would be up fro grabs from PPC – to social – to website and SEO concerns.

You could go all in on PPC – or you could do more website related stuff, and SEO – it really just depends on whether their marketing director wants sales NOW, or wants to slowly build a more long term minded slower burn approach with SEO.

Some numbers for those who just want to be told what to charge.

If you can't follow all of the above math and you're looking for where people are going to bite for website design and development projects in general – without doing a all of the aforementioned value calculation, when people are coming to a smaller agency or freelancer:

- Small to mid size marketing websites might land in between 5-10k
- Adding ecommerce or other significant functionality might put a site 10-17k
- Significantly customized websites – built from scratch and/or integrated with more API's etc. 17k up to infinite

Now these numbers are not what big ad agencies charge – but if you are someone who is working on your own or in a small agency, this is a common pricing range at the time of this writing.

 Can't I just charge what I want?

To be clear I know companies that don't do WordPress development projects for less than 250K – because they are only talking to large online publications where the website is literally the business.

I've also seen people theme a website for 1,000 bucks in the United States.

In fact, I touched several of these types of projects when I was just starting.

First of all, I wouldn't suggest you go this route if you were directing marketing for a company, but you can see how if you didn't own the client how this isn't the worst deal. 1k just to build something, if you know how – and you have a lot of these projects coming in – go for it.

The U.S. market has a lot more work for you if you're a WordPress developer here, so if you are good you'll likely move out of this lower number fairly quickly if you're well connected or you have leads coming in through whatever means.

 Some of pricing is really just trial and error

If you were just starting out, I would get whatever you could get to get better starting from free to 1,000 bucks to 2 or 3k.

If you are able to consistently pull in 2 or 3k – start pushing up from their and get 4-6k clients and once you gain your footing their push up to the next tier.

Of course ideally you want to own the design and the development of the site, not be working through some other middleman and be making upwards of 10k and beyond (what is it, 3k of that going to the government for taxes.)

But if you can't pull these numbers, or if you only do the development, understand that people maybe won't consistently give you 10k+ builds – you'll have to cut your teeth trying to be useful on whatever projects you can bring in.

You will sensitize yourself to the market = which is dependent on many factors

Businesses in the country or suburbs are going to have totally different expectations than those in the middle of the city – generally city businesses will be prepared to drop a lot more, because their used paying more for subjective things like 'taste' or 'perceived value.' I'm not saying this is either a good or bad thing, but in my process I do price in my taste so city oriented businesses might understand that a bit more.

 In the end it's pure economics – price goes up when demand exceeds supply

The thing that's a bit more subjective is quality.

Obviously you shouldn't overprice yourself if you don't have the necessary components yet to constitute high-quality services. You should cut your teeth on smaller companies and non-profits until you feel comfortable, but you also want to push that comfort for the good of your WordPress business.

 You want to push price up when you can so you can do your best work

"Price high, and justify," when you can get away with it, because it will allow you to have the room to create things of even higher value than the person paid. That's a good rule – try to exceed the clients expectations and what you sold by 25% every project so that if you sold a 10k website, make it feel more like a 12.5k website or higher.

This will raise the ceiling for what you're able to charge by filling your portfolio with work that could fetch those amounts in the future.

If you always do your best to exceed expectations on what **you are** able to sell, and this is the single biggest reason people will start breaking down your door to work with you.

So anyways, my experience – which might be somewhat outdated – was doing sites (with both design and development) for these levels – in order:

1st site: Non-profit $900

2nd site: Gym $2,000

3rd site: Non-profit FREE

4th site: Music venue $2,800

5th site: Small clock business $1,800

6th site: Bakery business $1,200

7th site: Church $1,400

8th site: Chiropractor $3,300

9th – 30th: Anywhere from $3,000 – $80,000 builds (higher number ones were done through agencies)

The highest number website I've done as an individual was around 30k and I would say in my experience at least there's somewhat of a ceiling there for what people are willing to pay to an individual – though I wouldn't be surprised if there are people making more than that out there as web designers.

There are definitely people positioned more as an agency feel that can consistently pull projects of that size or bigger. For WordPress sites though the pricing expectation depends so much on your location and the type of niche you occupy.

Are you the branding centric – high end designer / developer? Or are you the mom and pop shop? These types of aspects and perceptions definitely play in to how much a prospect will be willing to pay you to get a site built.

So what kind of businesses are good to go after?

 When you're first starting?

- Restaurants
- Music Venues
- Bands
- Non-profits
- Small shops
- Lifestyle bloggers

 When you've been around a couple years?

- Psychologists
- Construction Companies
- Contractors
- Landscaping companies
- Fashion
- Magazine

 After you're very experienced?

- Fashion industry companies
- Bigger editorial websites
- National / international food brands
- Pet food and pet industry brands
- Health niche companies
- Hospitals
- Other mid to high revenue companies from handmade products to national brands

It also may be very smart to position yourself, working as a subcontractor for agencies and forming agency partnerships. In my experience, working at an agency for 2 years and 8 months helped solidify my WordPress experience and work on bigger sites – and convince me what I am doing is valuable.

Some final thoughts on Pricing

Nothing is scientific about the above prices. But distilling down from the company you want to work with revenue by percentage and determining what amount might be allocated for digital marketing – their website – and subsequently the development of that website might be a good start. Their are always a hundred factors, but the strange thing is that price can actually be too low.

If people see that your services are priced half of the competition, what might they assume?

Keep this in mind when creating your proposals and **raise your prices.**

Now if you find that you can't find work and your last 8 proposals failed (might I suggest not sending a proposal unless you're 90% sure you'll get the job,) then perhaps move halfway back down to what you use to charge. But the entire point is to raise your prices so you can do better work, and offer a different experience – many people really are looking more at the value of what they are getting than strictly at price.

I love the service Bidsketch for proposals by the way, check that out and no matter what, find a way to whip up proposals quicker than 2 or 3 hours. With Bidsketch I got my first one done in an hour and every one since then is done in around 20 minutes – which is amazing.

CHAPTER TWELVE

MY STORY: GETTING STARTED WITH

WORDPRESS DEVELOPMENT

There was once a young kid, born in Robbinsdale, Minnesota and raised in a small town called Corcoran, Minnesota 20 minutes west of Minneapolis.

I was a dreamer – we didn't have a TV til I was 8 or 10 and I remember long summers playing ninja's on a blanket in our 2 acre yard after watching the movie 3 Ninja's in the theater, pretending our carpet was lava while my mom vacuumed, and our chores weeding and picking green beans.

 A pursuit of adventure, creativity and attention

Being the youngest of four brothers left me scrambling for attention behind them as they'd run up to our little forts in the wooded hill beside our house we called 'the weeds.' We pretended we were part of wars with fireworks or that we were pioneers or spies. My active imagination translated to my time at home too and I copied my brothers as they painted or made up cartoon characters with drawing.

My mom was a highly sensitive, intuitive woman and was really good at teaching us the general geometry of the human face as we sketched, and my dad provided the more mechanically minded, methodical approach that came off as a bit too stern to a sensitive boy who preferred his mom.

Getting attention for being creative, and the makings of a designer

Both of these things provide the backdrop for both my work ethic and my knack for trying to be wildly creative. I was rewarded with adulation when I brought my mom a finished story involving my cartoon character 'Bambu' who was a bumbling idiot who mostly messed things up, probably loosely modeled after Amelia Bedelia, a series of stories about a maid I loved growing up.

My brother John was second in his class and had done extremely well with sports, my brother Dan was a bit more timid but pursued a career as a sound engineer and is now building an 8+ million dollar a year company, and my brother Matt got into skateboarding and punk rock followed by evangelism and social media marketing.

I had no place to 'fit in' I felt, starting off.

All the roles were taken.

 ### Shenanigans

So I got into shenanigans, first as a Jackass style attention seeker – then as a burnout partier. All with the backdrop of loosely pursuing music. I'd draw and paint every once in awhile, but I wanted to be a rockstar.

After getting kicked out of the military, and then loosely flopping out of a church program for people trying to find their way in life – I partied again.

Then I hit a bottom. This was a pretty significant story that I won't get into in further detail, but suffice it to say that it provided the impetus to start something entirely new. I took of the heavy weight of needing to be the center of attention and gave myself permission to really work on my mental health.

Re-entering society – feeling I had something to prove

Now I was trying to find my place in society at 24 – after 6 years pursuing various possibilities including a lot of school and partying I still hadn't finished a degree and had a lot of credits for various pursuits that didn't really constitute a solid direction.

I knew I loved visual design and had a penchant for everything visual. So I started in with painting classes – then graphic design – then design + web development.

I took classes for HTML, CSS and then PHP and databases. I zero-ed in on WordPress development. I saw that I could at least roll out themes for people and then modify those themes with my CSS and HTML skills.

 The truth about the kinds of courses you'd want if you wanted to get into WordPress Development

- **HTML** – Simple and a more advanced class
- **CSS** – Simple and a more advanced class
- **PHP and Databases** – How they work and basics
- **WordPress specific PHP** – WordPress has some loops that are more specific to it – start learning about them, but understand to get started you only need to know the basics

Get started! The best way to understand what you'll need to know (and not to get trapped in an endless learning but not applying cycle) is to try to make a site ASAP.

For those that learn by doing (like me) I might even suggest starting before you even take courses.

The problem with taking 20 courses before you start working on a site (even just an experimental one) can sometimes make people who are more experiential learners that the task might be too big for them or that they need to keep learning forever.

Essentially, I'd err on the side of starting before you feel ready.

 A visual designer who knew code was the only way to really make something truly good and functional

In truth, I just wanted to be a visual designer, but I saw that the best finished websites had someone who understood how visuals transferred into code, and could code well at the helm

And so here I was, designing a bit – developing a bit – and looking for work. At first, the only clients I could find had smaller budgets, and so I couldn't afford to have a coder helping out. I got a couple clients and decided one day when the chef at the restaurant I was working at was swearing at me that I'd had enough.

 I walked out of my shitty restaurant job

All of the weight of my finances would rest on what was left of a small student loan and 2 clients whose websites I was finishing up.

Putting the weight on the new pursuit, in my case was probably one of the best things I possibly could have done. I pursued networking, learning, and making these sites as cool and effective as I possibly could to showcase in my portfolio with a new fervor.

 It was do or die time.

I still had a year of classes left, but I got an office for the summer and connected with people in any way I could to try to get work. I went to meet ups, connecting with as many people as I could on social media, and literally passed out fliers for my web design services – even when I went on a road trip to Yellowstone (and got a client!)

I think that my portfolio — however bad it'd seem if I looked at it now — was a huge part of why I was able to get work. I'd direct people to it, and it would give them a few examples of my work and my working philosophy, essentially. Which at the time was 'show what makes you special on-line,' and that's actually still pretty central to the way I present my unique value proposition today.

 Some people get really funny when you talk about portfolio's:

"You know, we're just so busy working on real client work to update our stuff."

Well that's all well and good when your portfolio is at least decent, but if you're plugging away at less than ideal clients and neglecting entirely the vehicle that's going to win you ideal clients, I'd say it'd be worth it to make time.

Don't take industry standards, or old catchphrases for granted — some of these are just bad habits, and marketing agencies and individuals have a lot of them.

 How I got my first job working at an agency

Like I said, I'd been going to meet ups and meeting as many people in the industry as possible — and I had also taken a paid internship one of my teachers at community college has suggested but few had pursued.

A connection I had made going to meet ups and then freelancing with, suggested talking to a smaller agency just outside the city called 'Snap Agency,' and I noted that. When the time came around to promote our portfolio show, I took one of the positions responsible for PR and used a guerrilla marketing tactic of bringing muffins to a bunch of agencies in town. I had also been taking 'informational interviews' with as many people who would have me as possible.

When I met up with Snap I brought muffins and talked about my connection with the friend / freelance acquaintance I had made at a meet-up.

As you can see – it was a lot of different factors that led to the connection finally being made.

 How I turned into a full-time freelance web designer and WordPress developer

I did a year and a half as a student / web designer and WordPress Developer, and then a 2 years and 8 months as a web designer and WordPress Developer / Marketing director at an agency – freelancing on the side.

After 4 years and 2 months of overlapping in these ways, I took the leap into full-time freelance. The trick was that I had been freelancing on the side for the 2 years and 8 months working at the agency with my boss's permission. It's smart to let your employee's do this as long as they're not competing with you on possible projects, as it sharpens their skills and enlarges their perspective.

By the time it felt appropriate to make the switch I had 4 side clients and had been studying the art of sales – but the biggest asset I can think of that enabled this all was doing search engine optimization on my own site. I had been writing deep guides in areas related to design and digital marketing and blogging regularly, as well as building links on other high authority websites to my personal portfolio timbdesign.com.

This discipline increased the authority of my website in Google's algorithm and people were coming to my site to learn about web design and other topics – but best of all when they were looking for 'Minneapolis web design' which has been huge for my business.

The basics of search engine optimization that made going full-time freelance possible, with 3 leads a week on average

I created high-value, deep content guides that brought people to my site for terms related to design and development and kept them reading – driving up the 'dwell time' on my site, and helped send signals to Google that my website has very valuable content.

I blogged around once a week to start, and then moved to blogging at least once per day this past year – every time I wrote a blog on my website, it essentially sends a signal to Google that my site is putting out fresh and relevant content to people looking for 'web design' related topics. Every time I do an article on other people's websites I help increase my website's authority with a link back and provide more brand awareness, so people know about me and learn about my services.

I did outreach to other websites and asked them if I could post on their site. I shared with them articles I had written before and promised to provide value to their audience. A good way to go about this is to first ask if they would like to see some possible titles for your post, and then review their blog and come up with a uniquely valuable article topic that fits in well with their existing content. Works like a charm.

I'd link back to my website in my bio or elsewhere in the article, and then also finding other ways to get links around the internet from high 'domain authority' websites. You can use a tool called 'Mozbar' to help you see what the domain authority for different websites you're on, and figure out which ones will be highly worth it to try to pitch a guest article to.

I've continued to tweak my meta-titles and descriptions with a WordPress plugin called Yoast to better suit the kinds of keywords I've started to get traffic for, submitted my sitemap to Google through their tool called 'Search Console' and monitored my top keywords with a paid tool called 'Ahrefs,' and made changes based on movements I see.

If all of this sounds a little exhausting, it sometimes is.

But the crucial piece is that even though it takes a lot of energy, I really deeply enjoy it. I love checking my keywords now, just like I love creating a fresh design and making it easy to use.

I like writing blog articles, just like I like coming up with unique article titles and writing deep guides for the audience to my web design blog.

You didn't always enjoy fresh spinach or other vegetables, remember? Sometimes you teach yourself to enjoy the things you know are good for your health — why not the health of your career, and the health of your business?

That's what I've strived to do, and I can say it's very worth it.

Last thoughts on getting started

If I had three next steps for someone that really wanted to get into WordPress development but didn't know how, these would be my five (pulled from the different categories of things I've discussed above).

1. Enroll in some kind of class for HTML. Ideally a community college for a coding class like HTML, or start by taking one course on Lynda.com for HTML — or CodeAcademy.

2. Take a challenge to code at least one website this month — no matter how basic. Only by learning and wanting to do something specific will you figure out the best thing to learn next.

3. Go to a WordPress meetup in your nearby city and get connected. If there's not a WordPress meetup nearby, go to a coding our UX meetup, or if there's none of these find someone near you that does these sorts of things and plan an intentional hangout to talk about this stuff.

It doesn't take 5,000 hours to get started – though it may take that much time to feel proficient, and another 5,000 to be closer to being an expert... but getting started today or taking the next step is the most important part of those 5,000 hours. I wish you the best of luck on your journey.

CHAPTER ELEVEN

SOME FINAL THOUGHTS – WAYS TO ROCK WORDPRESS
SITES FOR CLIENTS

Some final thoughts on 'WordPress Development for Noobs'

Writing this book has helped me recognize the value in my expertise, and I've had several people reach out and ask for help in learning WordPress development during the writing. My site is very targeted for WordPress design and development, so if someone searches for WordPress Minneapolis they'll likely see me. I do my best to help a little bit with every inquiry. WordPress is in demand, don't get it twisted – as of 2015, 50% of the top one million websites are powered by WordPress, and a lot of small to mid-size businesses are familiar with it. WordPress, as opposed to budget do-it-yourself website builders, is highly scalable, both with e-commerce sites under 1,000 SKU's (with WooCommerce) and an unlimited amount of organizational systems with custom post types, taxonomies and fields. If you do WordPress web development right, it's highly editable for clients as well – so study up and get busy.

Don't take my word for any of this – you don't really learn it until you implement in the wild:

This is all a start – the field manual to start you on a journey. But your ongoing learning process will be guided by your Google skills, Stack Overflow, and getting around other talented designers and developers on your way to mastery. In development, the key is settling in for the long haul. The more speed bumps you get over on your way, the less competition you'll have because half of the people who set out will turn back and take an easier profession. There's always the chance that you really are not well-suited for web development, but don't make that decision easily – because this stuff is tough for many, but worth it in the long run. The excitement will come in waves, as you jump one hurdle and see it working and feel the enjoyment of helping clients tell their story to the world. That's my story. One kid who started early, came up against the difficulty of finding his way, experienced hard-fought elation as he conquered the resistance and started being useful for people in this devotion to helping people and clients. The time has come when I'm doing my best to share these experiences and perhaps your life will be better for it, too. That's my hope.

 ## How to get more WordPress web design clients

It's not always easy when you're just starting out. I do think the best way to learn is to make websites for REAL THINGS, not imaginary concept websites that will get tossed to the side, and never face the pressure of real-world constraints. At least this has been my experience. Start with a non-profit, modify a simple basic theme, but always look for the thing that you bring to the table that other web designers/developers don't have. Look for that creative spark, that extra piece of value to make the project awesome.

If you find this individuality in your process, and start to emphasize it while you're selling your services, you'll have a lot more success gaining WordPress clients.

I'll go a little bit more into the story of my first four clients to give you an idea how one guy got started:

1. I offered to create an HTML version website for very cheap ($500 and an Ipad) to **my girlfriend's mother in law's non-profit.** It was quite a bit of work for not a lot of pay, but I got some much needed real-world experience.

2. Knowing I didn't want to have to make changes 10 times (on all the different templates) I wanted a CMS that made it easier to make sitewide changes, I connected with a friend of my girlfriend who owned a gym and offered my branding and web design help –

modifying a simple responsive theme. I focused on little delightful touches that would set the site apart from many generic websites.

3. I joined a promotion for a local culture magazine where I traded my web design services that they auctioned off for $6,000 worth of advertising. I made an advertisement that emphasized my commitment to thinking outside the box and getting to the bottom of what makes people special (my differentiation is being a marketing consultant as well), and got two new clients by running the ad. One was a local music venue – **I biked and bussed to that appointment, wiping off sweat on my way in. I told the person I was meeting with I was somewhat fresh to this but was 100% committed to making it worth it for them.**

4. The other client I got from this ad was a antique clock dealer and craftsman – who understood that I was new to web design and development as well, and was super encouraging because he was a single owner/operator and was adamant I would love freelancing. I was realizing that creating value for clients as an entrepreneur could be a legitimate business pursuit, with good energy coming from those I was working for, even if I felt a little fresh to the venture sometimes.

 Your story may be totally different, but hustle will be your friend. Go one step beyond the competition to get one more level of success.

Yes, you're competing with all the other web designers and developers in your area. This may not matter as much when you've been around for a little while, have 10–20 websites under your belt, testimonials to prove successful and positive results – but in the meantime, you have to work hard. I'm not the guy who's going to tell you I have an algorithm to implement and you get to sit back and chill because that just isn't my story. I worked longer hours than a lot of the people that were trying to do the same thing as me, and some of them are baristas three years later.

Nothing against service industry jobs – but that's not where I'd be the most fulfilled. Those people likely get to get off work and go home and watch TV without even thinking about work again. That's not what it's like in my experience in web design and development when you're hustling hard. I don't resent it at all, I work harder and get more opportunities to do what I consider real, extremely useful, and powerful work that helps the businesses I'm assisting make more money and tell their story visually and in an interactive way.

To me, that's bad-ass. I'll take a little trade off of some work while other people are playing. I like my job, so work/life balance to me is ying and yang, not either/or.

 10 Quick ways to get more WordPress / web design clients now:

• **Talk with your friends and family,** let them know you can help them if they need a website.
• **Post something on Facebook** letting people know you're fresh and looking to help people with creating websites.
• **Go to your local meetups** (meetup.org is a good place to start,) UX – WordPress – Web Design – etc, and let people know you'll be their cheap minion to learn more.
• **Google the top 20 WordPress web designers** in your city and ask each if you could offer free work in exchange to learn as much as you can from them.
• **Change your other social media profiles** to briefly explain that you're looking for web design clients.
• **Write on a blog** (ideally connected to a portfolio) where you can share the things you're learning.
• **Look at local newspapers** and culture magazines for places to advertise cheaply, and create an ad that emphasizes what makes you different.
• **Reach out to local small businesses** you admire personally, try to make a meeting with their owner or the marketing decision maker.
• **Talk with people you know in the marketing or web design industry** – see if you can be the person they give referrals to when

they are too expensive for a client.
*   **Talk to other designers and developers** if you know any, and see how they got clients. Let them know you can be helpful when needed.

How to create an alignment of expectations and positive testimonials and reviews

The most important thing in all of this for stoking business? It's not to get as many clients and pop out as many websites as possible. It's to curate a history of clients who loved what you did. You need to be able to get a positive testimonial from as many clients as you can, so focus on that as the outcome and not just getting the site done. This requires clear communication about what the expectations are on both sides:

*   Be clear about what your process is. Maybe it's (Meetup, Design and development, Revision, Launch,) or (Discovery, Architecture, Design, Revision, Development, Revision, Launch) but you need to be able to share this as soon as you start finding your rhythm.
*   Let them know they get two revisions after design, three revisions in development, or whatever those numbers are, because this kind of clarity put in the work order or proposal will save you a lot of headaches later.
*   I would go so far as to say exactly what the website design and development process will include as far as functionality in the proposal. Doing this for me has allowed me to create a "change order" when something wasn't in the proposal. I cannot tell you how important this has been for me in reducing 'scope creep,' the bane of web designers' existence. Start now – **include functional requirements – in the proposal** that you both sign and agree to formally.

All of this might seem a little 'hard' or formal, especially if you are doing a website for an acquaintance (ideal to move away from doing websites for friends and family as soon as you can), but it actually just sets you up with clear expectations and allows you to be more relaxed with everything else. If there's two revisions in the work order, you can say, "I'd love to add a new custom post type" (let's say press or something) "that will take some time and is not part of the existing agreement (but I'd love to help with it) – it would just be an extra $500, would you like to add it?}

It's a super positive thing, trust me. If you just do something you didn't agree to before, you'll resent the person you're doing the work for – and that's not fair to them or you. Make expectations crystal clear as much as you can, keep on refining this process to your liking as you put out more proposals, and you'll have it down after you experience any friction from not properly scoping things out a couple times. In the end, still always aim for making sure the client is a raving fan at the end of the process so you can procure those testimonials and reviews, and you can feel great about the whole experience.

I feel obligated to tell you all is not sunshine and roses. Some clients are a pain in the ass (sorry clients) and you have to live and learn. A great majority of my projects for clients have been very positive, but expect that you will have some issues that occasionally pop up when money is exchanged for services. Aligning expectations as much as possible helps, but you will learn more lessons and some of them hurt. Be prepared for that and stay resilient, and do your best to stay positive. Success is how many times you pick yourself back up, dust yourself off and live to help another client create an awesome website.

 Signing off, and thank you for reading.

Thank you for reading this.

I'm happy if I even helped one person on the way to greater financial peace of mind, as WordPress web development has brought me, and a greater sense of being able to practically help people with their businesses. The biggest asset I have is my website, as it brings in 500 visitors a day and a good 3 client opportunities a week at the time of this writing.

Share your work with the world, put out content to help your tribe, connect with people on social, and write for other bloggers like you to get more visibility for your site.

You can check out my podcast "It's a Code World" on iTunes – the first episode is about getting found on Google for designers and digital marketers and it will help you on that journey as well.

Don't be shy – please tweet me and @timbdesignmpls if any of this was helpful to you, and reach out if you need anything to tim@timbdesign.com